T0318955

Cambridge Elements ≡

Elements in Applied Social Psychology
edited by
Susan Clayton
College of Wooster, Ohio

SELVES AS SOLUTIONS TO SOCIAL INEQUALITIES

Why Engaging the Full Complexity of Social Identities Is Critical to Addressing Disparities

Tiffany N. Brannon
University of California, Los Angeles

Peter H. Fisher
University of California, Los Angeles

Abigail J. Greydanus
University of California, Los Angeles

CAMBRIDGE
UNIVERSITY PRESS

CAMBRIDGE
UNIVERSITY PRESS

University Printing House, Cambridge CB2 0DS, United Kingdom

One Liberty Plaza, 20th Floor, New York, NY 10006, USA

477 Williamstown Road, Port Melbourne, VIC 3207, Australia

314–321, 3rd Floor, Plot 3, Splendor Forum, Jasola District Centre,
New Delhi – 110025, India

79 Anson Road, #06–04/06, Singapore 079906

Cambridge University Press is part of the University of Cambridge.

It furthers the University's mission by disseminating knowledge in the pursuit of education, learning, and research at the highest international levels of excellence.

www.cambridge.org
Information on this title: www.cambridge.org/9781108812733
DOI: 10.1017/9781108874267

© Tiffany N. Brannon, Peter H. Fisher and Abigail J. Greydanus 2020

First published 2020

A catalogue record for this publication is available from the British Library.

ISBN 978-1-108-81273-3 Paperback
ISSN 2631-777X (online)
ISSN 2631-7761 (print)

Selves as Solutions to Social Inequalities

Why Engaging the Full Complexity of Social Identities Is Critical to Addressing Disparities

Elements in Applied Social Psychology

DOI: 10.1017/9781108874267
First published online: September 2020

Tiffany N. Brannon
University of California, Los Angeles

Peter H. Fisher
University of California, Los Angeles

Abigail J. Greydanus
University of California, Los Angeles

Author for correspondence: Tiffany N. Brannon, tbrannon@ucla.edu

Abstract: Social disparities tied to social group membership(s) are prevalent and persistent within mainstream institutions (e.g., schools/workplaces). Accordingly, psychological science has harnessed *selves* – which are malleable and meaningfully shaped by social group membership(s) – as *solutions* to inequality. We propose and review evidence that theoretical and applied impacts of leveraging "selves as solutions" can be furthered through the use of a ***stigma and strengths framework***. Specifically, this framework conceptualizes selves in their fuller complexity, allowing the same social group membership to be associated with stigma, risk, and devaluation *as well as* strengths, resilience, and pride. We provide evidence that by enacting policies and practices that (a) reduce/minimize ***stigma*** and (b) recognize/include ***strengths,*** mainstream institutions can more fully mitigate social disparities tied to inclusion, achievement, and well-being. Using social groups that vary in status/power, we examine implications of this framework including the potential to foster positive, recursive, and intergroup impacts on social inequalities.

Keywords: diversity, mainstream institutions, power/status, social disparities, social identity, stigma, strengths

ISBNs: 9781108812733 (PB), 9781108874267 (OC)
ISSNs: 2631-777X (online), ISSN 2631-7761 (print)

Contents

1 Overview

I know that I was a different man at the end of the plague of AIDS than I was at the beginning, **just as so many gay men and many others were** . . . . You have a choice: to submit to fear and go under, or to live with the virus and do what you can. **And the living with it, while fighting it, is what changes you over time; it requires more than a little nerve and more than a little steel** . . . . I know also that the **AIDS epidemic, more than any other single factor, transformed the self-understanding of gay men and lesbians** . . . . Within a couple of decades, out of the ashes, we had marriage equality, a new world of visibility and toleration.

- Andrew Sullivan, 2020 (emphasis added)

> Out of the huts of history's shame
> **I rise**
> Up from a past that's rooted in pain
> **I rise**
> I'm a black ocean, leaping and wide,
> Welling and swelling I bear in the tide.
> Leaving behind nights of terror and fear
> **I rise**
> Into a daybreak that's wondrously clear
> **I rise**/ Bringing the gifts that my ancestors gave,
> **I am the dream and the hope of the slave**.

- Maya Angelou, 1978 (emphasis added)

These opening excerpts highlight perspectives related to psychological selves – encompassing an individual's self-construal, motivation, and behavior – in the context of social identities and social inequalities. Specifically, the quotes underscore links between self-understanding and meaning tied to profound and long-term oppression such as the HIV/AIDS epidemic and its impact on LGBTQ+ (lesbian, gay, bisexual, transgender, queer +) individuals and slavery and related systems of subjugation and their effect on Black/African Americans. Taken together, the perspectives reflected in the written words of Sullivan and Angelou highlight that social groups like LGBTQ+ individuals and Black/ African Americans are not merely, or passively, marked by stigma and related negative consequences of oppression. Rather, the excerpts highlight that such social groups are also shaped in meaningful ways by such collective hardships and experiences; they are shaped in ways that foster resilient optimism ("I rise . . . I am the dream and the hope of the slave") and require the resolve of strength ("it requires more than a little nerve and more than a little steel").

This Element builds on these insightful perspectives to motivate the importance, both theoretical and applied, for researchers, leaders, and policy makers alike, of conceptualizing social identities and social inequalities in a fuller complexity. Specifically, we highlight the potential to leverage the complexity in the psychological self that allows social identities to be associated not only with *stigma* but also, and relatedly, with *strengths*. We conceptualize stigma as the more direct experience of oppression. As such, stigma often serves to relegate marginalized groups like LGBTQ+ individuals and Black/African Americans to lower power and status positions that are associated with enduring and adverse consequences and conditions (e.g., Goffman, 2009; Major & O'Brien, 2005). We conceptualize strengths as active, adaptive, and creative responses to the negative consequences and conditions tied to stigma. As such, strengths can serve as resources that can buffer and protect against the determinantal consequences and conditions linked to stigma.

As captured in Figure 1, stigma and strengths are closely related yet not completely overlapping. That is, as illustrated by Sullivan's words in the opening excerpt, strengths can develop in response to the conditions and consequences created by stigma. For instance, having to contend with stigma and related oppression can fuel grit, determination, and resilience (e.g., "And

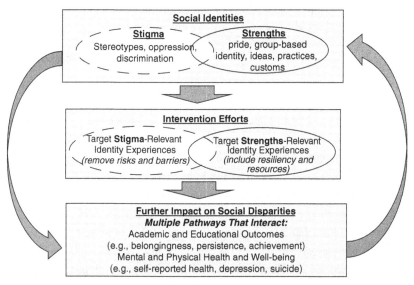

Figure 1 Stigma and strengths approaches to addressing social disparities. As depicted by the recursive arrows, social identities and social disparities are meaningfully linked. Intervention efforts that target social identities and how those social identities are tied to stigma and strengths are able to leverage the fuller complexity of those identities. Whereas, as shown by the dotted lines, approaches to social identities and intervention efforts that only target stigma are often effective yet can be incomplete, especially with regard to furthering impacts on social disparities.

the living with it, while fighting it, is what changes you over time; it requires more than a little nerve and more than a little steel"; see also Crocker & Major, 1989; Rivas-Drake et al., 2014a, 2014b; Sellers, Chavous, & Cooke, 1998). Yet, strengths can be harnessed by social groups with long-standing experiences of oppression through sources that extend beyond collective, contemporary, and/or historical experiences of marginalization. For instance, one source of resiliency that has been shown to buffer and dampen the negative effects of stigma and oppression on Black/African Americans is cultural interdependence. Accordingly, a sense of feeling connected with and close to other racial/ethnic ingroup members as well as to ideas and practices associated with one's own racial/ethnic ingroup has been associated with resiliency effects in academic and well-being outcomes among Black/African Americans (e.g., Brannon & Lin, 2020; Brannon, Markus, & Taylor, 2015). Cultural interdependence associated with Black/African Americans has multiple roots. For example, it can stem from collective responses to oppression and marginalization, and it also can be traced to African cultures and proverbs that emphasize strength tied to a collective understanding of the self (e.g., West African proverbs like "I am because We are, and because We are therefore I am" and "If spiders unite, they can tie up a lion" (Boykin, Jagers, Ellison, & Albury, 1997; Mbiti, 1970; Nobles, 1991).

We integrate and build on insights tied to stigma as well as strengths associated with social identities and social inequalities to introduce a **stigma and strengths framework**. We propose and review evidence that a stigma and strengths framework can empower mainstream institutions to further intervention efforts to mitigate social disparities. That is, we reveal benefits that can be harnessed among historically disadvantaged groups and across social group lines to include socially dominant groups by enacting policies and practices that (a) reduce or minimize stigma and related adverse consequences and (b) recognize or include strengths and related advantageous consequences. Such policies and practices seek solutions that are twofold. On the one hand, they eliminate stigma – stereotypes, discrimination, and other negative identity experiences that mark difference tied to social identity, in ways tied to being devalued and excluded. And, on the other hand, they promote strengths – positive ingroup connections, pride, and other positive identity experiences that mark difference, tied to social identity, in ways tied to being valued and accepted. We examine theory and applied implications of stigma and strengths approaches using social groups that vary in status/power (e.g., racial/ethnic minorities, sexual orientation minorities, and racial/ethnic and gender dominant group members), and we discuss the potential for such approaches to foster positive and recursive impacts on social inequalities.

2 Background: Motivating the Current Framework

> When I first arrived at school . . . I was a little overwhelmed and a little isolated. But then I had an opportunity to participate in a three-week, on-campus orientation program that helped me get a feel for the rhythm of college life. And once school started, I discovered the **campus cultural center, the Third World Center**, where I found students and staff who came from families and communities that were similar to my own . . . . And if it weren't for those resources and the friends and the mentors, I honestly don't know how I would have made it through college. But instead, I graduated at the top of my class, I went to law school – and you know the rest.
>
> -Michelle Obama, 2014 (emphasis added)

> When I got to Princeton, I saw right away that a sense of belonging would not come easily. The community was much bigger than any I had known, bound by its own traditions, some of them impenetrable to women and minorities. And so I found my place where I could, working with **Acción Puertorriqueña and the Third World Center.**
>
> – Sonia Sotomayor, 2013, p. 256 (emphasis added)

Social identities tied to racial/ethnic minority groups such as being Latino/a/x or Black/African American have long been linked to social inequalities in a variety of consequential life domains including educational access, attainment, and achievement (Ashkenas, Park, & Pearce, 2017; Levy, Heissel, Richeson, & Adam, 2016). Accordingly, social psychological approaches aimed at understanding and mitigating social inequalities in education, for instance, have prominently focused on social identities. Many of these approaches have considered how such social identities tied to membership in a racial/ethnic minority group can be associated with stigma, threat, and other vulnerabilities that can undermine a sense of belonging as well as academic persistence and performance (Steele, 2011; Walton & Cohen, 2007, 2011). Yet, as illustrated by the excerpts in which former first lady of the United States Michelle Obama and Associate Justice Sonia Sotomayor recount their lived experiences as an African American and Latina American student, respectively, at Princeton University, the links between their social identities and the adverse social and academic experience of not feeling a sense of belonging are complex.

That is, both Obama and Sotomayor give voice to a lived experience in which their social identities are meaningfully tied to uncertainty about belonging, as a *problem* yet also as a *solution*. Thus, reflecting well-documented social disparities, their personal experiences echo extant findings in which Latino/a/x and Black/African Americans are at risk for experiencing belongingness uncertainty as well as perceiving academic settings as unwelcoming (Benner & Graham, 2011; Mendoza-Denton, Downey, Purdie, Davis, & Pietrzak, 2002;

Walton & Cohen, 2007). However, their personal narratives also highlight that the same social identities, which are linked to risk, can be associated with securing a sense of belonging through engagement with cultural centers and campus organizations (i.e., Third World Center, which was renamed the Carl A. Fields Center for Equality and Cultural Understanding, and Acción Puertorriqueña). Obama and Sotomayor link cultural centers and campus organizations, which are characteristically inclusive of ideas and practices tied to Latino/a/x and Black/African American culture, to providing connections to others and a sense of belonging. Research also upholds their personal reflections by showing the potential for participation in practices and organizations associated with racial/ethnic minority groups to promote belongingness and in turn a myriad of positive academic and health outcomes (e.g., Brannon et al., 2015; Brannon & Lin, 2020, in press; Rheinschmidt-Same, John-Henderson, & Mendoza-Denton, 2017).

This Element proposes and reviews evidence that selves can serve as powerful solutions to social inequalities. It furthers the insight that this potential tied to selves can be especially evident when theory-based intervention efforts to address disparities take the fuller complexity of social identities into account. The excerpts from Obama and Sotomayor highlight the complex implications of social identities tied to racial/ethnic minority group membership. In particular, in those excerpts, Obama's and Sotomayor's social identities are depicted as a source of stigma yet also a source of resilience or strengths. In the context of social groups with long and enduring histories of oppression and discrimination, we theorize that the experience of contending with stigma, prejudice, and other negative identity-relevant experiences can foster collective, group-based, adaptive, and creative responses. We theorize that these collective responses to oppression and discrimination that reflect historical and persistent shared experiences can encourage resilience and a sense of positive connection or interdependence with others who share the social identity; it can be a source of strengths.

Thus, in contrast to stigma that is characterized as a source of difference that can signal by virtue of social group membership that an individual is devalued (Goffman, 2009; Major & O'Brien, 2005), we conceptualize strengths as a source of difference that can signal by virtue of social group membership that an individual is valued. We also conceptualize strengths as contrasting with stigma in its consequences – that is, while stigma is often associated with negative consequences, strengths can be associated with positive consequences. This conceptualization of strengths tied to social groups that are stigmatized is consistent with research on racial/ethnic identity. Such literatures have noted that racial/ethnic identity is multidimensional (Sellers, Smith, Shelton, Rowley,

& Chavous, 1998; see also Phinney & Ong, 2007), and that it can reflect various aspects of daily life. Accordingly, racial/ethnic identity can reflect experiences of discrimination, cultural socialization practices in homes or religious institutions, and engagement with media and customs that celebrate and affirm shared experiences, and it can offer definitions of group membership that are positive and counter-stereotypical (Hughes et al., 2007; see also Markus, 2008; Taylor, Brannon, & Valladares, 2019). And, aspects of racial/ethnic identity such as racial pride, private regard, and racial centrality have been shown to be associated with advantageous, rather than adverse, social, academic, and health outcomes (Shelton, Yip, Eccles, Chatman, Fuligni, & Wong, 2005; see also Kiang, Yip, Gonzales-Backen, Witkow, & Fuligni, 2006). For instance, in a meta-analysis Rivas-Drake (2014) and colleagues found that aspects of racial/ethnic identity tied to feeling a sense of positive affect connected to group membership (i.e., "happy," "good," "proud") are significantly associated with outcomes linked to success and thriving across a number of academic and well-being outcomes among adolescents (e.g., lower depressive symptoms, greater academic achievement).

Further, we theorize and review evidence that a stigma and strengths framework can extend to sexual orientation minority groups. The following excerpt from Anthony Venn-Brown's autobiography *A Life of Unlearning – A Journey to Find the Truth* (2007, p. 306, emphasis added) in which he reflects on his social identity as a gay man exemplifies collective responses to oppression and discrimination associated with group-based pride among sexual orientation minorities:

> When you hear of Gay Pride, remember, it was not born out of a need to celebrate being gay. It evolved out of our need as human beings to break free of oppression and to exist without being **criminalized, pathologized or persecuted**. Depending on a number of factors, particularly religion, freeing ourselves from gay shame and coming to self-love and acceptance, can not only be an agonising journey, it can take years. Tragically some don't make it. Instead of wondering why there isn't a straight pride be grateful you have never needed one. Celebrate with us.

Venn-Brown's words highlight numerous social disparities tied to possessing a social identity as a sexual orientation minority member (i.e., "criminalized," "pathologized," "persecuted"). He even acknowledges disparities tied to suicide (i.e., "tragically some don't make it"); the Centers for Disease Control and Prevention (CDC) and other national- and state-level surveys report that sexual orientation minority youth are two to three times more likely to contemplate suicide than their heterosexual peers (Perez-Brumer, Day, Russell, & Hatzenbuehler, 2017; Strauss, 2019). Venn-Brown's words also proclaim the importance of Gay Pride as a collective response that is linked to asserting a sense of humanity, "self-love and acceptance." His words explicitly place celebrations of Gay Pride in the context of oppression and discrimination, including within mainstream institutions (i.e., "religion"), and in so doing he makes salient an adaptive need to be resilient and thrive despite such factors.

Moreover, Venn-Brown's words underscore a distinction between social identities tied to long-standing and historic disadvantage and those that are associated with advantage, power, and status. That is, he suggests that individuals who identify as "straight" (e.g., a socially dominant group compared to sexual orientation minorities) do not share the explicit need for "pride" practices, and he invites such individuals to "celebrate" with those that do (e.g., to show allyship). Aligned with these insights, the Element examines the fuller complexities of stigma and strengths tied to the social identities of groups that have endured persistent oppression and discrimination (i.e., racial/ethnic and sexual orientation minority groups), and it also engages an intergroup perspective. It contrasts and reviews complexities tied to social groups that have been historically dominant and privileged (i.e., White Americans as a racial/ethnic majority group and men as a gender dominant group). It also highlights the implications for socially dominant groups, to borrow Venn-Brown's words, of "celebrating with" disadvantaged groups or taking part in cultural ideas and practices associated with racial/ethnic and sexual orientation minority groups.

3 Current Framework: Toward a Stigma and Strengths Approach

Society is plagued by pervasive social disparities, which reflect intergroup inequalities across several consequential life domains. For instance, in the United States there are historical and consistent racial/ethnic achievement gaps in education; gender, salary, and leadership disparities in organizations; and sexual orientation inequalities in health (Graf, Brown, & Patten, 2018; Lee, 2002; Lyness & Grotto, 2018; Meyer & Northridge, 2007). The prevalence and persistence of such disparities reflect complex social issues and underscore the need for solutions that can mitigate disparities in "wise," precise and strategic, and enduring ways (Walton & Wilson, 2018; see also Dixon, Levine, Reicher, & Durrheim, 2012). Leveraging an integrated social psychological approach to identity and interventions, we theorize and review evidence that the psychological self when conceptualized and engaged in its fuller complexity can provide powerful solutions to social inequalities. Specifically, we highlight the potential to leverage the complexity in the psychological self that allows the same identities to be associated with both stigma and strengths. Thus, the same social identity when tied to a source of stigma or a source of strengths can foster nearly polar opposite consequences – some adverse and undesired and others advantageous and valued – for daily life experiences as well as cumulative and intergenerational life outcomes (Brannon & Lin, 2020; Markus, 2008).

3.1 Overview of Sections

In the sections that follow, we first review research that examines social identities associated with low power/status groups that have an enduring history of contending with stigma and negative stereotypes and are often the targets of prejudice and discrimination. We provide evidence that approaches to reducing social disparities experienced by Latino/a/x and Black/African Americans as well as sexual orientation minority individuals that focus on stigma are efficacious yet incomplete (see Figure 1, which references stigma-only approaches and Figure 2).

Whereas approaches that focus on stigma as well as strengths, that more fully conceptualize and engage such social identities as tied to risks and resources, have the potential to benefit efforts to mitigate social inequalities in a number of ways (see Figures 1 and 3). Such approaches can directly benefit members of low power/status groups as well as incite positive intergroup implications that can further address and sustain reductions in social disparities (see Figures 4 and

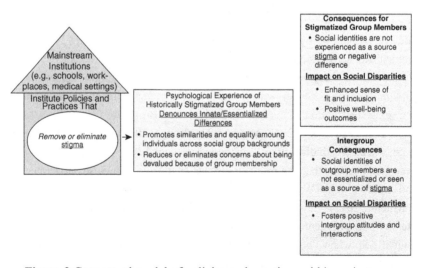

Figure 2 Conceptual model of policies and practices within mainstream institutions that target stigma. Such stigma approaches can have critical impacts on social disparities by affecting outcomes associated with stigmatized group members and across intergroup lines.

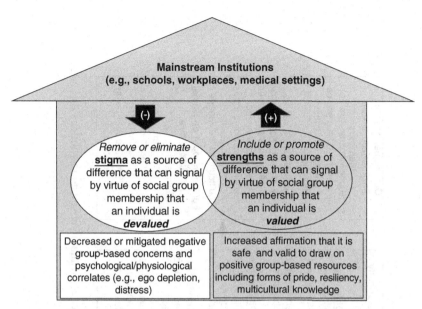

Figure 3 Mainstream settings leveraging stigma and strengths approaches. Applying stigma and strength approaches can impact social disparities through multiple pathways. As depicted, for example, such approaches can reduce negative consequences tied to social and cognitive resources that are adversely impacted by stigma and stigma-related experiences (e.g., distress) that undermine academic and well-being outcomes. Additionally, such approaches can increase or reveal positive consequences tied to social, cultural, and cognitive resources (e.g., resiliency, multicultural knowledge) that can promote thriving in academic and well-being outcomes.

5; Brannon, 2018; Brannon et al., 2015; Brannon, Taylor, Higginbotham, & Henderson, 2017; Brannon & Walton, 2013). Throughout, we discuss the implications for mainstream institutions of using stigma approaches (Figure 2) versus stigma and strength approaches (Figures 4 and 5).

Then, we review research that examines social identities associated with high power/status groups; we focus on whiteness and masculinity. We highlight that while power/status often creates meaningfully different needs and functions tied to stigma and strengths, it is fruitful for interventions aimed at reducing social disparities to consider a stigma and strengths framework in the context of socially dominant identities (e.g., whiteness and masculinity). For instance, although men relative to women are socially dominant and are associated with higher status and privilege, men do experience stigma and social disparities that can have adverse intra- and intergroup consequences. Hence, masculinity can be tied to stigma or stereotypical and narrow constructions that limit

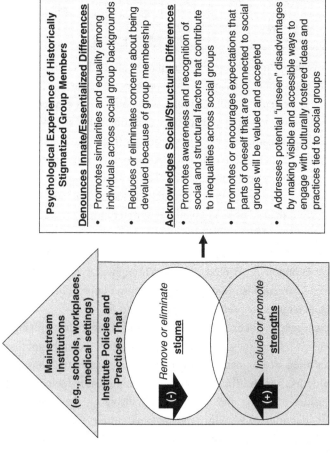

Figure 4 Consequences for stigmatized group members of policies and practices within mainstream institutions that target stigma and strengths

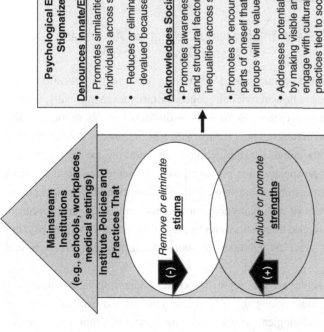

Figure 5 Intergroup consequences of policies and practices within mainstream institutions that target stigma and strengths

Mainstream Institutions (e.g., schools, workplaces, medical settings) **Institute Policies and Practices That**

Remove or eliminate stigma (-)

Include or promote strengths (+)

Psychological Experience of Historically Stigmatized Group Members

Denounces Innate/Essentialized Differences

- Promotes similarities and equality among individuals across social group backgrounds

- Reduces or eliminates concerns about being devalued because of group membership

Acknowledges Social/Structural Differences

- Promotes awareness and recognition of social and structural factors that contribute to inequalities across social groups

- Promotes or encourages expectations that parts of oneself that are connected to social groups will be valued and accepted

- Addresses potential "unseen" disadvantages by making visible and accessible ways to engage with culturally fostered ideas and practices tied to social groups

Intergroup Consequences

- Social identities of outgroup members are not essentialized or seen as a source of **stigma**

- Social identities of outgroup members are recognized as a positive source of pride, connections and **strengths**

Further Impact on Social Disparities

- Fosters positive intergroup attitudes and interactions

- Cultivates intergroup allyship or awareness of and willingness to address structural inequalities experienced by stigmatized groups emotional expressiveness and/or that fuel dismissiveness and sexist behaviors and attitudes, behaviors and attitudes that in turn have the potential to inflict both ingroup and intergroup harm (e.g., detrimental health and well-being outcomes for men as well as women; Courtenay, 2000; Swim, Hyers, Cohen, & Ferguson, 2001). However, interventions that seek to reduce such harmful effects that fail to recognize the fullness of masculinity – that only conceptualize it as a source of stigma or devalued identity – are likely to be met with reactance and backlash (Brannon, Carter, Murdock-Perriera, & Higginbotham, 2018; Fisher & Brannon, in prep). In contrast, intervention efforts that operationalize masculinity in a fuller complexity – by seeking to address its link to stigma but also its association to strengths or as a potentially valued identity that can shape affect, motivation, and behavior – can minimize or eliminate such backlash and thus lead to consequences that can mitigate social disparities. Finally, we underscore that engaging a stigma and strengths approach among high power/ status groups has the potential to promote awareness of privilege and to encourage allyship – attitudes and behaviors on the part of dominant group members that can further the mitigation of social disparities (Droogendyk, Wright, Lubensky, & Louis, 2016). It also has the potential to make visible sources of misunderstandings that can impede efforts to address social inequalities (see Brannon et al., 2017).

3.2 Why Selves Are an Efficacious Target for Addressing Social Disparities

Several persistent and pervasive social disparities (e.g., wealth, education, well-being gaps) are tied to how individuals, contemporarily and historically, interact with, access, and experience mainstream institutions such as schools, workplaces, or medical settings. Thus, mainstream institutions are critical sites for intervention efforts aimed at mitigating such enduring social disparities. Aligned with this perspective, the Element proposes that policies and practices within mainstream institutions are especially well positioned to impact consequential social issues by harnessing a stigma and strengths approach. Specifically, we suggest that a stigma and strengths approach can allow psychological selves to serve as solutions to social disparities that are wise and multifaceted.

Psychological selves are efficacious targets for addressing social disparities. Selves can shape motivations and behavior in implicit and explicit ways. For instance, social psychological research has shown that interventions that invoke a sense of identity by merely phrasing important civic behavior like voting as a noun (i.e., "voter") instead of an action (i.e., "voting") increase motivation to vote and actual voting behavior in field experiments (Bryan, Walton, Rogers, & Dweck, 2011). In the context of contending with stigma, selves are especially attuned to settings within mainstream institutions that can signal different identity contingencies such as threat or inclusion or a valuing of diversity (Purdie-Vaughns, Steele, Davies, Ditlmann, & Crosby, 2008). Research has demonstrated that cues in school settings that signal threat (e.g., gender under-representation in science, technology, engineering, and mathematics (STEM), racial stereotypes) can undermine a variety of inclusion and even physiological outcomes (e.g., sense of belonging, domain and career interest, physiological indicators of threat and vigilance; Murphy, Steele, & Gross, 2007; Williams et al., 2019). Conversely, school settings that signal a valuing of diversity in their mission statements have shown an association with positive physiological outcomes such as lower inflammation and other cardiometabolic health benefits for their students (Levine, Markus, Austin, Chen, & Miller, 2019).

Given these features of psychological selves – as shapers of motivations and behaviors and as attuned to cues in mainstream settings that signal an affirmation of stigma (e.g., threat, stereotypes) or strengths (e.g., valuing of diversity) – we theorize that mainstream settings can powerfully intervene to impact social disparities by leveraging a stigma and strengths approach. The proposed application of such an approach in mainstream settings is shown in Figure 3. Although studies that demonstrates the need for intervention efforts to decrease stigma and its consequences and those that advocate for the urgency of intervention effects to promote strengths and its consequences are often examined in separate literatures (see Brannon et al., 2017; Brannon & Lin, 2020) we highlight the benefits of doing both. That is, we theorize that policies and practices within mainstream institutions that seek both to reduce stigma and to promote strengths can create environments that combat social disparities through multiple pathways (see Brannon & Lin, 2020).

As depicted in Figures 1, 3, and 5, a stigma and strengths approach would allow individuals from social groups that are stigmatized to feel safe from the threat of being seen through the lens of stereotypes and stigma, which has been shown to promote an array of social inequality-attenuating outcomes (e.g., academic achievement and persistence, social and health well-being; see Steele, 2011; see also Spencer, Logel, & Davies, 2016; Yeager & Walton, 2011). And, it would allow individuals from such social groups to feel safe to draw on strengths tied to social identity and related lived experiences that serve as a resource – a source of pride, resiliency, and even multicultural knowledge. Drawing on and engaging with such strengths tied to social identities that are also stigmatized have been shown to also promote outcomes tied to mitigating social inequality (Altschul, Oyserman, & Bybee,

2006; Caughy, O'Campo, Randolph & Nickerson, 2002; Chavous, 2000; Cokley & Chapman, 2008; Ethier & Deaux, 1994; Fente & Fiske, 2018; Fuligni, Witkow, & Garcia, 2005; Hughes et al., 2006; Rivas-Drake et al., 2014a, 2014b; Sellers et al., 1998; Spencer, Noll, Stoltzfus, & Harpalani, 2001; Smith & Silva, 2011).

Several characteristics of psychological selves – the fact that they are dynamic and malleable and that they implicitly and explicitly shape motivations and behaviors – make them particularly efficacious for intervention efforts within mainstream settings. That is, targeted efforts to address social inequalities must be sustainable and demonstrate a recursive impact on outcomes tied to disparities. For instance, an intervention effort to address health disparities by impacting dietary habits must influence, directly and/or indirectly, dietary choices and consumption behaviors repeatedly, over time and not just at a single time point (e.g., healthier food choices for a single meal). Similarly, meaningful changes to educational outcomes require improved and/or maintained achievement and persistence over time and across a variety of academic settings (e.g., positive academic outcomes that generalize to multiple academic courses and not just a single course or a particular class meeting). Thus, interventions that invoke the self and recursively impact processes tied to the self can impact motivations and behaviors in sustainable and lasting ways (Walton, 2014; Walton & Wilson, 2018; Yeager & Walton, 2011). **This potential of the self and its links to motivations and behaviors highlight the need for a stigma and strengths approach to addressing social disparities. That is, even a mainstream setting that is free or relatively free from stigma can impact the selves of individuals from stigmatized groups in ways that undermine motivations and behaviors tied to mitigating inequality.**

3.3 Potential Limitations of Stigma (versus Stigma and Strengths) Approaches

A stigma and strengths approach, one that recognizes social identities as a source of stigma and strengths, has the potential to address "unseen" or "hidden" disadvantages that stigma approaches can allow to remain invisible and subsequently unaddressed. For example, social group membership as an individual from a working-class (versus middle-class) background is a stigmatized group identity (Johnson, Richeson, & Finkel, 2011; Stephens, Markus, & Fryberg, 2012). Like other stigmatized identities, it has been associated with negative psychological consequences including distress and concerns about fit within mainstream settings. However, the lived experience of individuals from working-class backgrounds is complex. It is not characterized solely by a relative lack of material resources or by occupying status positions of relatively less power or rank (Kraus, Piff, & Keltner, 2011; Stephens & Townsend, 2013). It is also characterized by collective, creative, adaptive responses to stigma as well as constraints and limitations imposed by the material, subjective, and objectives realities tied to being from a working-class background (Brannon & Markus, 2013; Stephens et al., 2011; Stephens, Hamedani, Markus, Bergsieker, & Eloul, 2009). Among individuals from working-class backgrounds, research within social and cultural psychology has illuminated collective responses associated with *interdependence* – a relative prioritizing of connections to others in understandings of the self, including motivations and behaviors (Snibbe & Markus, 2005; Stephens, Markus, & Townsend, 2007). Thus, interdependence is one strength associated with individuals from working-class backgrounds.

Further, interdependence associated with being from a working-class background also tends to reflect a conjoint sense of agency in which actions reflect taking others into account versus making decisions that reflect autonomous or decontextualized preferences (Stephens, Fryberg, & Markus, 2011). Thus, in working-class contexts (e.g., neighborhoods, communities) interdependence and conjoint agency are sources of strengths and resilience. They afford adapting and thriving in spite of relatively limited resources. An example of interdependence and conjoint agency as an adaptive and creative response comes from the late, acclaimed musician Ray Charles's autobiography in which he shares the following reflection on his upbringing (Charles & Ritz, 2004, p. 155): "Affluence separates people. Poverty knits 'em together. You got some sugar and I don't; I borrow some of yours. Next month you might not have any flour; well, I'll give you some of mine." Charles's personal reflection underscores a sense of interdependence – reciprocal cooperation and giving that can allow physical needs such as food staples like flour and sugar to be met despite limited direct personal access to such items. Charles's words also highlight interdependence as a strength that can help individuals overcome the need to access material resources like sugar or flour; thus, consistent with the present framework, it is a strength that is tied to stigma and disadvantage.

Although interdependence and conjoint agency can foster thriving within working-class contexts, a series of experimental and field studies by Stephens and colleagues has shown that interdependence and conjoint agency can fuel "unseen disadvantages" within college and university settings (Stephens, Fryberg, Markus, Johnson, & Covarrubias, 2012; see also Stephens, Dittmann, & Townsend, 2017). That is, despite common policies and practices within college and university campuses that often proclaim a commitment to increasing access and degree attainment among individuals from working-class backgrounds, these settings are associated with cultural mismatches in which individuals who have more independent understandings of the self and use more disjoint models of agency (i.e., behaving and acting in ways in which the autonomous self including individual preferences are dominant and primary) are advantaged. Such independent understandings of the self and disjoint models of agency tend to be more prevalent among individuals from middle-class backgrounds in countries like the United States.

Moreover, experimental interventions have demonstrated that seemingly small changes that allow colleges and universities to be perceived as settings that value and affirm interdependence and conjoint agency can facilitate enhanced academic achievement and sense of fit among individuals from working-class backgrounds. Small changes have included acknowledging interdependent motivations and decision making (e.g., desire to use college degree to give back to others in a community, decision to attend the college or university as a joint decision between an individual student and their close others) in college or university admissions and acceptance materials, or even having panel discussions in which speakers explicitly note how a sense of interdependence and conjoint model of agency has shaped their experiences – both challenges and opportunities (Stephens, Hamedani, & Destin, 2014). Moreover, leveraging strengths tied to an interdependent understanding of self and conjoint model of agency among individuals from working-class backgrounds has been shown to benefit social outcomes in health and workplace settings (Stephens, Markus, & Fryberg, 2012; Stephens, Markus, & Phillips, 2014).

Taken together, a stigma and strengths approach has potential to harness the psychological self in powerful ways to address social disparities. Yet, maximizing this potential requires taking into account the fuller complexity of selves tied to long-standing inequality (e.g., racial/ethnic minorities, individuals from working-class backgrounds) by employing intervention efforts to reduce stigma and risk and to promote strengths and resilience. Importantly, a stigma and strengths approach highlights that policies and practices that solely seek to address stigma and its consequences are vulnerable to fueling and reproducing inequality by allowing mainstream settings to uphold, as demonstrated by Stephens and colleagues' work on addressing social class disparities – "unseen disadvantages." Hence, even an academic setting, for example, that seeks to minimize stigma by having practices and policies in place to deter and discipline discrimination can still signal negative, stigma-relevant messages about social groups like racial/ethnic minorities or sexual orientation minorities. That is, if such an academic setting employed efforts to reduce stigma (e.g., explicitly did not tolerate discrimination) yet had curriculum practices that excluded the perspectives or representations of non-dominant groups, that setting would still be at risk for signaling messages that differentially associated some social groups with value and higher status. It could signal by the omission and invisibility of the perspectives and representations of nondominant groups that those social groups are not valued and relegated to lower status (see Fryberg & Eason, 2017; Salter et al., 2018; see also Figures 4 and 5).

Additionally, racial/ethnic minority group members, whose sense of self is often shaped in meaningful ways by their group membership, remain vulnerable to not experiencing a fuller sense of fit and not thriving in mainstream settings, even settings that are free or relatively free from stigma. Motivations and behaviors that are central to such individuals' sense of self, if not visibly reflected or supported within mainstream settings, may not be seen as congruent with identification with the setting and thus foster reduced engagement or even withdrawal from the setting (see Schmader & Sedikides, 2018).

Finally, selves are efficacious for suggesting solutions to address social inequalities among historically disadvantaged as well as advantaged social groups. Mainstream settings are inherently interdependent, requiring involvement and participation across individuals from a variety of social backgrounds. Thus, to achieve intended goals it is crucial for intervention efforts to avoid backlash and to promote buy-in across individuals within a given mainstream setting. A stigma and strengths approach offers insights related to leveraging selves tied to historically advantaged social groups including motivations and behaviors in ways that minimize negative reactance or backlash and foster buy-in (see Brannon et al., 2018).

3.4 Power/Status Differences in How Stigma and Strengths Shape Social Identities

The author of the book *So You Want to Talk About Race,* Ijeoma Oluo, opens her manuscript with a personal narrative in which she notes the profound ways in which race has shaped her life. She begins by sharing a reflection that highlights stigma and negative identity-relevant experiences tied to her race/ethnicity. She writes (2019, pp. 5–6, emphasis added):

> When I was a young child it was the constant questions of why I was **so dark** while my mom was so white – was I adopted? Where did I come from? When I became older it was **the clothes not cut for my shape** and the **snide comments about my hair and lips** and the teen idols that would never ever find a girl like me beautiful. Then it was the **clerks who would follow me around stores** and the **jobs that were hiring until I walked in** the door and then they were not. And it was the bosses who told me that I was **too "loud,"** the **complaints that my hair was too "ethnic" for the office,** and why, even **though I was a valued employee, I was making so much less**

money than other white employees doing the same job. It is the **cops I can't make eye contact with,** the Ubers that abandon their pickup, driving on instead of stopping when they see me. When I had my sons, it was the **assumptions that they were older** than they were, and that their roughhousing was **too violent.** It was the **tears they came home with** when a **classmate had repeated an ignorant comment of their parents.**

Oluo's recollection underscores how her experiences tied to her race/ethnicity have been linked to stigma in ways that explicitly marked her as different and devalued. The author eloquently traces this marked devalued difference back to her childhood and weaves it forward to her experiences as a parent of sons who are also forced to contend with prejudice and discrimination tied to race. Specifically, she recounts that she endured "constant questions" about her "dark" complexion relative to her mother, and she bears witness to her young sons being seen through the lens of stereotypes such as being "violent" or "older." She also shares her experience of consoling her sons, who are described as in "tears" in response to interracial interactions with peers who have shared hurtful comments passed down from the peers' parents. Negative race-related experiences like the ones Oluo recounts can occur throughout the life course (Priest, Paradies, Trenerry, Truong, Karlsen, & Kelly, 2013; Spears & Bigler, 2005), and such experiences, and the consequences for health and well-being, can be intergenerational (Gibbons, Gerrard, Cleveland, Wills, & Brody, 2004; Novak, Geronimus, & Martinez-Cardoso, 2017). Like Oluo's description of her children hearing negative race-related comments that their peer(s) had learned from their parents, research demonstrates significant associations between children's intergroup attitudes and those of their parents (see Degner & Dalege, 2013 for a meta-analysis of more than 45,000 parent-child dyads that finds medium effect sized associations between intergroup attitudes of parents and their children).

Further, Oluo's reflection on the ways in which race has shaped her life underscores that racism, discrimination, and exclusion occur routinely and through everyday interactions with a range of institutions (e.g., transportation services ("Uber"), retail facilities, workplaces) and individuals (e.g., "bosses," "cops," strangers). Resonating with her words, research and theorizing within psychology have shown that such negative race-related experiences are deeply embedded within institutions and across a variety of interpersonal interactions (e.g. Markus & Moya, 2010; Salter, Adams, & Perez, 2018). Additionally, and consistent with Oluo's recollection of her experiences, such negative experiences can be subtle and institutional or structural (e.g., pay inequalities) and can reflect individual attitudes (Henkel, Dovidio, & Gaertner, 2006; Nier & Gaertner, 2012; Pincus, 1996).

Consistent with a stigma and strengths framework, Oluo's words in the introduction for her book voice a complexity to her social identity tied to race/ethnicity. Specifically, she expresses the complexity of recognizing that her race/ethnicity, while linked to stigma, has also meaningfully shaped her life in adaptive and positive ways that have fueled a sense of pride and valued connection to other racial/ethnic ingroup members. Thus, as the current framework proposes, her social identity tied to race/ethnicity is not solely defined by negative race-related experiences. Reflecting complexity, Oluo shares how her race/ethnicity which is a source a stigma, is also a source of strengths (2019, pp. 6–7, emphasis added):

> But race has also been **countless hours spent marveling at our history**. Evenings spent **dancing and cheering to jazz and rap and R&B. Cookouts with ribs and potato salad and sweet potato pie**. It has been **hands of women braiding my hair**. It has been **reading the magic of the words of Toni Morrison, Maya Angelou, and Alice Walker and knowing that they are written for you**. It has been **parties filled with Jollof rice and fufu and Nigerian women wearing sequin-covered gowns and giant geles on their heads**. It has been **the nod to the black stranger** walking by that says, **"I see you fam."** It has been **pride in Malcolm, Martin, Rosa, and Angela**. It has been a room full of the most **uninhibited laughter** you've ever heard. It has been the touch of my young son as he lays his hand over mine and says **"We're the same brown."**

Aligned with research on cultural ideas and practices tied to racial/ethnic identity, Oluo's words paint a portrait of her race/ethnicity as shaping experiences in her life in rich, multifaceted ways that involve "history," traditions tied to food like "ribs," "potato salad," and "sweet potato pie," hair-breading customs, and music (Ramsey, 2003; Sellers et al., 1998). Importantly, many traditions tied to the cultural heritage of racial/ethnic minority groups like Black/African Americans have roots that have been meaningfully shaped by the need to adaptively and creatively respond to discrimination and oppression (for elaborated examples, see Brannon et al., 2015; Brannon et al., 2017). Yet, the cultural heritage of such groups and the present-day traditions and practices tied to that heritage do not only reflect responses to negative race-related experiences; they also reflect cultural survival and represent traditions and practices that can be traced to African cultures in the case of African Americans (Holloway, 2005; see also Boykin et al., 1997; Jones, 2003).

Moreover, her recounted, positive race-related experiences also record personal engagement with Black/African American literature through acclaimed authors like Toni Morrison, Maya Angelou, and Alice Walker. Further, she shares the experience of reading Black/African American literature and feeling a sense of positive connection or interdependence with the authors' words (e.g., "knowing that they are written for you"). Her words also note a sense of interdependence with "black strangers" and actions of symbolic solidarity shown between ingroup members (e.g., nod "that says, 'I see you fam'"). And, almost poetically, the same skin color that has been source of stigma – an explicit marking of devalued difference – Oluo recalls, in the excerpt, how it has also been a source of similarity as she shares a loving moment with her son in which he proclaims, "We're the same brown." Experiences of positive connection with ingroup members, like the ones so vividly penned by Oluo, have been associated with strengths or a variety of advantageous life outcomes among racial/ethnic minority group membership including across the life-span (e.g., Hughes et al., 2006; Rivas-Drake et al., 2014a, 2014b; Sellers et al., 1998; see also Tatum, 2017).

Taken together, both excerpts from Oluo underscore that the same social identity such as being a racial/ethnic group member can be a source of both stigma and strengths. Section 4 Resistance to Stigma Can Foster Strengths (Pride) among LGBTQ+ Individuals, we review evidence and propose that a similar framework of identity complexity can apply to sexual orientation minority groups. In so doing, we call attention to critical similarities that can be harnessed to benefit social interventions, and we also note differences in the lived experiences and related insights for how such social identities can be more fully leveraged to address social disparities. Like the excerpts from Oluo that highlight intersectionality tied to lived experience of being a race/ethnic minority (e.g., multiracial, multinational, gender identities), we also underscore intersectionality associated with sexual orientation minority groups.

While meaningfully different, an important underlying commonality that we emphasize in the social identities tied to racial/ethnic minorities and those of sexual orientation minorities is the function of pride or strengths in relation to stigma and the enduring experience of discrimination and oppression. We theorize that, more broadly, social groups that have a sustained experience of discrimination and oppression can adaptively draw strengths from a sense of positive connection to other ingroup members and through knowledge of their ingroup's collective history (Taylor et al., 2019). The cultivation of such strengths and pride, although reflecting multiple sources, importantly reflects the shared endurance and understanding of oppression and discrimination. And like Oluo's personal reflection, these lived experiences of both pride and prejudice or stigma and strengths shape how individuals from these groups understand the self. These lived experiences also shape interactions with ingroup members and across social group lines and within mainstream institutions (Brannon et al., 2015; Brannon & Lin, 2020).

Thus, a unifying similarity between racial/ethnic minorities and sexual orientation minorities is the experience of nondominance or occupying relatively low status and/or power positions. For socially dominant groups such as White Americans in US society, lived experiences tied to social group membership are drastically different from those of nondominant group members. This point is captured by Robin DiAngelo (2016) in *What Does It Mean to Be White?: Developing White Racial Literacy*: "Because **whites are not socialized to see ourselves collectively**, we don't see our group's history as relevant. Therefore, we expect people of color to trust us as soon as they meet us. We don't see ourselves as having to earn that trust"(p. 203, emphasis added). Thus, as articulated by DiAngelo, the socialization experience of White Americans carries with it the privilege of being free from the weights and at times the constraints of imposed interdependence or having to understand oneself through the "collective" lens of a broader group (Markus, 2017). As DiAngelo states, this freedom, this independence and ability to conceive of oneself as an autonomous individual have intergroup implications (Brannon et al., 2017; Taylor et al., 2019). One consequential intergroup implication is cross-group misunderstandings and relatedly drastically different perspectives and expectations tied to trust.

Notably, this intergroup implication is only revealed or made visible when White American identity is examined in a fuller complexity. That is, it is examined not only as a source of privilege and at times stigma (e.g., threat of being seen through the lens of stereotypes tied to racism) but also as a multifaceted set of experiences that includes socialization practices (e.g., how White Americans are taught to think about the self in relation to their racial/ethnic ingroup and its history). Such revelations tied to social identity and intergroup differences (e.g., perspectives, socialization, trust) can yield intervention insights. For example, it could suggest ways to reduce reactance or backlash against information about social inequalities by helping dominant group members take the perspectives of and/or experience empathy with nondominant group members. Such intervention insights could be especially helpful when information about social inequalities might require dominant group members to shift from thinking about themselves as autonomous individuals to being part of a larger collective group. In the same book, DiAngelo (2016) describes such reactions:

> **group consciousness**, whites often respond **defensively when grouped with other whites**, resenting what they see as **unfair generalizations**. **Individualism prevents us from seeing ourselves as responsible for or accountable to other whites** as members of a **shared racial group that collectively benefits from racial inequality**. (p. 200, emphasis added)

The type of reaction or reactance described by DiAngelo in this excerpt can be a significant barrier to addressing social inequalities, especially when intervention efforts are tied to structural or systemic solutions. Accordingly, viewing social disparities through a context of individualism renders historical and structural forms of discrimination and oppression invisible, while making primary the intent of discrete individuals. And, since behaviors in the context of individualism represent individual preferences, it makes discrimination and oppression the act of individuals who are "bad actors" or individuals who are inherently prejudiced. All of these implications of an individualistic view of social disparities can fuel well-documented racial/ethnic group differences in perceptions of inequality and historical knowledge of past inequality (Nelson, Adams, & Salter, 2013; Parker, Horowitz, & Mahl, 2016; see also Bonam, Nair Das, Coleman, & Salter, 2019). It can also foster a lack of appreciation and understanding of perceived discrimination or microaggression experiences of nondominant group members that may reflect impact versus the explicit intent of an individual or institution (Sue, 2010; Sue et al., 2007; Sue et al., 2019).

One way to counter or guard against individualistic understandings of social inequalities is to promote and support policies and practices within mainstream institutions that allow dominant group members to learn about the history and lived experiences of nondominant group members. Thus, mainstream settings that have policies and practices in place that reduce and address stigma are creating environments in which differences tied to marking certain individuals by virtue of group membership as devalued are not tolerated and regarded as not valid. As much research has shown, this is important for mitigating a variety of social disparities (Steele, 2011; see also Figure 2). Yet, a stigma and strengths approach goes even further by recognizing the importance of minimizing or eliminating negative sources of difference tied to stigma while also recognizing and including sources of difference tied to strengths. Importantly, doing both, minimizing stigma and recognizing strengths, has potential to benefit members of nondominant groups (see Figure 4), and it has the potential to benefit intergroup outcomes (see Figure 5). In addition to the social, academic, and health benefits already reviewed in this Element, it can afford access to dual or multicultural identities for nondominant group members. (The implications of a stigma and strengths framework for dominant group members is explored more deeply in Section 5 Making the Invisible Visible: Examining Dominant Group Identities in Context that explicitly focus on white[*] identity and masculinity.)

---

[*] The use of capitalization for the term "white" is an evolving and debated issue; there are valid and important reasons to capitalize and not capitalize the term. In this Element, we are not using the terms "White American" and "white" interchangeably, although the two terms are related and encompass some shared meaning. "White American" refers to a social and cultural group within the United States. Thus, we capitalize "White American(s)" to be consistent with norms in which terms that reference social and cultural groups are capitalized. The term "white" refers more often to a socially constructed racial group. To be consistent with many of the texts that we cite in reference to "whiteness" or "white" racial identity, we do not capitalize the term.

For example, stigma and strength approaches can allow Black/African American students to cultivate a broader or mainstream identity alongside an African American identity within a given school setting (see Brannon et al., 2015). Cultivating and supporting such dual or multicultural identities can offer members of nondominant groups a greater sense of inclusion within mainstream settings. Across social group lines, stigma and strengths approaches can help nondominant group members appreciate sources of differences that make visible systemic and structural inequalities. It can also be associated with increasing support for policies and practices within mainstream institutions that address those inequalities (Brannon & Walton, 2013; see also Brannon, 2018).

3.5 Broadening the Framework: Other Minority and Dominant Groups

In brief, approaches to intervening to address social disparities that leverage the psychological self are especially well positioned to create "wise" or lasting and enduring change. Such approaches have the benefit of drawing on and mobilizing often recursive, yet malleable, motivations and behaviors tied to the self. However, such approaches can leverage greater power and maximize intervention benefits by taking into account the fuller complexity of the self. In particular, policies and practices within mainstream institutions can further and advance intervention efforts by reducing stigma (taking into account how social identities associated with oppression and discrimination can be linked to risk, vulnerabilities, and adverse consequences) and recognizing strengths (which has the potential to address "unseen" sources of disadvantages and to include perspectives and representations of nondominant groups that can foster positive consequences including a sense of inclusion and promotion of intergroup support). The current stigma and strengths framework acknowledges the importance of stigma approaches yet notes that such approaches can be enhanced and advanced by also considering strengths. Building on the research reviewed about racial/ethnic minorities, in the sections that follow we apply this stigma and strengths framework to social identities associated with sexual orientation minority and dominant groups.

4 Resistance to Stigma Can Foster Strengths (Pride) among LGBTQ+ Individuals

There is no such thing as a single-issue struggle because we do not live single-issue lives. Malcolm knew this. Martin Luther King, Jr. knew this. Our struggles are particular, but we are not alone.

– Audre Lorde, February, 1982

Audre Lorde delivered this statement as part of a Malcom X celebration weekend at Harvard University. As a Black lesbian, feminist theorist and poet, Lorde understood the importance of recognizing intersectionality tied to social issues, especially those that impact LGBTQ+ (lesbian, gay, bisexual, transgender, queer +) individuals. The following section on LGBTQ+ identity mirrors Lorde's embracing of intersectionality to highlight the multifaceted nature of lived experiences associated with LGBTQ+ individuals. Aligned with a stigma and strengths approach, we underscore how taking such complexities into account can further intervention efforts aimed at mitigating social disparities linked to this social group.

Although LGBTQ+ individuals represent a myriad of intersectional identities that vary along dimensions of power, status, and privilege, forces (e.g., social norms, laws) and experiences create common struggles and hardships among individuals whose sexuality or gender identity are marked as deviant or stigmatized (Moleiro & Pinto, 2015). Like racial/ethnic minorities, LGBTQ+ individuals have historically demonstrated active, adaptive, and creative collective responses to oppression and discrimination, thus, allowing the experience of identifying as a LGBTQ+ group member to be tied to sigma yet importantly to also be linked to strengths. Understanding how identity functions in this social group as a source of stigma and strengths, we theorize and review evidence, as well as provide critical insights related to rallying ingroup and also outgroup support. We propose that such elaborated understanding can help address a number of social disparities and can be especially beneficial for mitigating inequalities associated with inclusion and mental health outcomes (which have a severe impact on LGBTQ+ individuals; Valdiserri, Holtgrave, Poteat, & Beyrer, 2018).

An appreciation of how LGBTQ+ individuals have endured stigma yet have also responded and developed strengths can readily be seen in many LGBTQ+ individuals' resistance to policies and practices within mainstream institutions that fostered identity concealment. The cultivation of strengths among this social group is also evident in acts of community building that have provided needed support and at times buffered the negative experiences associated with restrictive policies and practices within mainstream institutions. For example, as early as the 1950s there are documented examples of community organizing associated with LGBTQ+ identity. These efforts often included demands for inclusion within the US society. Accordingly, organizations like the Mattachine Society, which was one of the earliest LGBT organizations in the United States, have historically promoted the belief that being gay, for example, did make an individual different; however, this difference could be used to empower homosexuals with unique internal resources to fight against injustice (Marche, 2019).

Membership in a sexual orientation minority group is often concealable. Accordingly, for many LGBTQ+ individuals the decision to make their social identity visible is often construed as an individual choice. This decision has been described as being "in" or "out" of the closet. The choice of whether to conceal or disclose can have profound personal and mental health consequences (e.g., concealing can be negatively related, whereas disclosing can be positively related to psychological well-being; Douglass, Conlin, & Duffy, 2020; Nouvilas-Pallejà, E., Silván-Ferrero, P., Fuster-Ruiz de Apodaca, M. J., & Molero, F. 2018). Thus, such characteristics and consequences of identity concealment have parallels with the experiences of racial/ethnic minorities and identity management strategies that are sometimes employed by individuals to gain acceptance into mainstream institutions. For instance, Black/ African Americans in the United States have been theorized and shown to experience double-consciousness and to engage in code-switching behaviors (DuBois, 1903; see also Bell, 1990; Brannon et al., 2015; McCluney, Robotham, Lee, Smith, & Durkee, 2019). And, historically, in response to restrictive laws in the United States (e.g., Jim Crow) that explicitly denied access and resources to people of color, some African Americans have engaged in racial passing (Hobbs, 2014).

The fight for equal rights of LGBTQ+ individuals started out, in part, from a necessity to survive. That is, many individuals were unable to conceal their identity as easily as those who were cis-gendered, and straight passing (Levitt, 2019). Such experiences that made one's social identity as an LGBTQ+ individual visible also created greater vulnerabilities for discrimination. Aligned with such realities, many early pioneers and leaders for LGBTQ+ rights have been women who held intersectional identities like Marsha P. Johnson, Silvia Rivera, and Audre Lorde. The experience of all these women is incredibly and notably diverse, and yet each of them recognized the importance and strength of community. They also recognized the importance of cultivating pride tied to their identities and making representations of that pride tied to their identities visible within mainstream society. They harnessed such pride tied to their identities to fight against injustice and outgroup prejudice. For example, in 1970 Marsha Johnson and Silvia Rivera founded an organization to provide material support to transgender individuals (e.g., housing for homeless individuals) called STAR. In a 2002 essay that was later published in 2013, Rivera reflected on that organization and the importance of resistance and visibility:

> We raised a lot of hell back when STAR first started, even if it was just a few of us. We ate and slept demonstrations, planning demonstrations. We'd go from one demo to another the same day. We were doing what we believed in.

And what we're doing now, the few of us who are willing to unsettle people and ruffle feathers, is what we believe in doing. **We have to do it because we can no longer stay invisible. We have to be visible. We should not be ashamed of who we are.** We have to show the world that we are numerous. There are many of us out there. (Rivera 2013, p. 54–55, emphasis added)

Rivera's words, like the stigma and strengths framework, capture the distinctions of visibility (Brannon et al., 2015; Markus, 2008). On the one hand, stigma by definition creates visibility; it is a marking of individuals and social groups in ways that signal lower status or being devalued. Yet, Rivera's words highlight that while stigma marks individuals and social groups, the solution is not invisibility or unmarking; rather, it is marking or visibility in ways that denounce shame tied to, for instance, identification as a LGBTQ+ individual. This type of visibility tied to pride can serve as a source of strengths, one that like the research reviewed on racial/ethnic minority social groups and noted in Rivera's words can have positive consequences for ingroup members and across intergroup lines (e.g., "the world").

4.1 Institutional Inclusivity: Insights of a Stigma and Strengths Framework for Belonging

Due to fear of discrimination, many LGBTQ+ individuals have hidden who they are and only recently have begun to be more open and vocal about their identity. Such shifts can be attributed in part to changes in policies and practices within mainstream institutions including laws put in place in some, though not all, states (Gleason et al., 2016; Movement Advancement Project, 2019). These shifts have allowed LGBTQ+ individuals to express their identity without explicit fear of discriminatory repercussions. One example of this is whether an LGBTQ+ individual feels they can be open about their identity at work, and the job satisfaction and level of anxiety that may come with either concealing or sharing this part of one's self (Griffith, & Hebl, 2002; Wessel, 2017).

Much of how an individual feels when it comes to disclosing their sexual identity in the workplace has to do with the ally support of others in the setting (e.g., co-workers), as well as inclusive organizational policies (Wessel, 2017). Notably, these factors that promote disclosure can be transmitted, taught, and cultivated through interventions efforts that target broader institutional groups to lower LGBTQ+ individuals' anxiety and promote satisfaction and well-being (Griffith & Hebl, 2002). Although not the explicit focus of a large survey (n=379) of gay and lesbian employees, Griffith and Hebl examined the association between specific types of workplace policies and practices and sexual orientation minority employees' disclosure behavior. They found that specific policies and practices that target stigma such as having a written nondiscrimination policy or offering diversity training that directly addresses issues that impact gay and lesbian individuals were positively associated with disclosure behavior. And, consistent with a stigma and strengths framework, they found that specific policies and practices that target strengths such as recognizing gay and lesbian employee organizations and supporting activities for gay and lesbian as a social group were also associated with disclosure behavior. Taken together, such findings highlight the potential efficacy of both stigma- and strengths-related policies and practices within mainstream institutions. Parallel to such findings, research by Brannon and Lin (in press) has shown policies and practices that target "pride and prejudice" can have separate, yet beneficial, effects on inclusion and in turn achievement and well-being within college and university settings among racial/ ethnic minorities.

When it comes to affirming gender identity, the use of correct pronouns and chosen name (a signal of visibility and acceptance) across all gender identities can contribute to a significant reduction in depressive symptoms, as well as suicidal ideation and behavior among transgender youth (Olson, Durwood, DeMeules, & McLaughlin, 2016; Russell, Pollitt, Li, & Grossman, 2018). These findings suggest the importance of looking further into the implementation of institutional policies and practices that encourage broader outgroup affirmations of individuals' gender identity. Items like the inclusion of pronouns in one's email signature, regardless of gender identity, or the sharing of pronouns at the beginning of a class might uniquely signal inclusion to transgender individuals. Along these lines, past studies have shown physiological health advantages among students of color who attended schools that emphasized the value of diversity (Levine et al., 2019). Thus, such efforts that recognize strengths might also play an important role in the experience of LGBTQ+ identity and its consequences (e.g., health and well-being), particularly among transgender individuals. Moreover, laws that impact institutional policies and practices, such as state bathroom bans, have also played a role in recent feelings of fairness and inclusivity among transgender individuals. Given the observed positive association between recognizing and affirming identity among LGBTQ+ individuals, it is possible that the implementation of these laws and the unavailability of accommodations like gender-inclusive bathrooms may signal unfairness to members of this community and foster negative inclusion and well-being outcomes (Chaney & Sanchez, 2017; Seelman, 2016; Wernick, Kulick, & Chin, 2017. Examples like the lack of bathroom access, improper use of pronouns, and other markers of discrimination produce excessive anxiety unique to transgender individuals in comparison with their cis-gendered peers (Becerra-Culqui et al., 2018; Gülgöz et al., 2019).

While past studies have shown the importance of emphasizing similarities between groups for significant shifts in opinions about marginalized and stigmatized goals (Lytle & Levy, 2015), recent studies have shown how the sharing of cultural differences can also produce significant changes in attitudes among outgroup members. This work has shown that contact that involves engagement with strengths (e.g., cultural ideas and practices) associated with marginalized and stigmatized groups can also positively shift support for policies and practices that help marginalized individuals (Brannon, 2018; Brannon & Walton, 2013, Page-Gould, Mendoza-Denton, & Troop, 2008). Altogether, such findings emphasize the importance of creating accurate and complex representations – ones that mitigate stigma and make visible strengths in media and other outlets (Gomillion, & Giuliano, 2011; Li, 2019; Reimer et al., 2017).

With recent television shows in the United States like *Pose* and *Orange Is the New Black*, there is the emergence of such representations that portray LGBTQ + identity in its full complexity. That is, both shows cast transgender actors to play characters with plotlines that uplift the stories and performances of transgender women of color. The shows also include historically positive representations of intersectional, traditionally marginalized identities. Consistent with research on intergroup contact, which underscores the importance of exposure to and engagement with cultural differences, these shows and this type of representation have the potential to bridge gaps between social groups. They also have the potential to expose and educate outgroup members on the individual lives and experiences of people they may otherwise never come into contact with, possibly affecting their future policy choices and support for LGBTQ+ individuals (Broockman, & Kalla, 2018). Further, there is also potential for LGBTQ+ individuals to find support and strength in these positive representations (McInroy & Craig, 2015). Hence, it is important to look at how representation in various media outlets not only promotes positive feelings toward social groups, such as LGBTQ+ individuals, but can also become a catalyst for both ingroup and outgroup members to actively support the rights of stigmatized and marginalized community members (Jones & Brewster, 2017; Swank, Woodford, & Lim, 2013).

4.2 How Technology and Social Media Can Reduce Stigma yet Recognize Strengths

Throughout history, often out of sheer necessity and frequently through the use of new technologies, LGBTQ+ individuals have discovered ways of finding one another, building their complex view of self. Thus, over time, LGBTQ+ individuals, like other stigmatized groups, have expanded their collective ability to engage in interdependence and collective action by using their social identity to combat social inequalities (Brannon, Markus, & Taylor, 2015; Fox & Ralston, 2016). As a whole, the LGBTQ+ community's known history is much newer than that of many other identities. This is in large part because of a lack of documentation over the course of time, as it was historically easier for society as a whole to dismiss this group, making it difficult for LGBTQ+ individuals to find one another and connect as a group with shared goals and interests (Bronski, 2011). Even now, the history and needs of LGBTQ+ individuals, at times, falls to the wayside and is rendered invisible through policies and practices that create barriers to recording characteristics like correct gender markers on documents. Such factors have also served as obstacles for researchers and others to take into account how unique the experience of this social group may be in comparison to other social groups (Coulter, Kenst, Bowen, & Scout, 2014; Smalley, Warren, & Barefoot, 2016).

One of the ways in which outgroup members have had contact with, been educated on, and affirmed identities of LGBTQ+ individuals has been through the boom in technology as a method of communication. Sexual orientation, gender identity, and gender expression often remain aspects of an individual's identity that need to be shared for outgroup members to know when they may be interacting with someone who identifies as LGBTQ+ (Griffith & Hebl, 2002). This makes spaces like social media particularly important, as such spaces can have social norms that encourage people of all genders and sexual orientations to share aspects of their identity that they may not have otherwise spoken about in a face-to-face interaction. When both people from nondominant groups, as well as people from dominant groups, share these parts of their identity, such as sharing their pronouns, they normalize these acts and make it easier for individuals from traditionally stigmatized groups to talk about their identity and feel supported (Fox & Ralston, 2016; Russell, Pollitt, Li, & Grossman, 2018). This sharing of identities has also made it easier for LGBTQ+ individuals to connect with one another.

Websites like YouTube, Tumblr, and Twitter have allowed LGBTQ+ individuals to utilize markers, such as hashtags, to search for one another and join together in online groups where they share and celebrate one another's identity (Cavalcante, 2018; Drushel, 2010; Fink & Miller, 2013; see also Jackson, 2017). This is especially important when outside gathering places, such as bars, that cater specifically to LGBTQ+ individuals appear to be dwindling in numbers, increasing the importance of community members connecting online (Jenzen, 2017; DeHaan, Kuper, Magee, Bigelow, & Mustanski, 2013; Pinto, Melendez, Spector, & 2008). Online spaces have also given many people the opportunity to explore aspects of their identity that they may not yet be comfortable sharing with the broader world (Cannon et al., 2017; Webster, 2019). This is especially true for transgender individuals who may use the Internet not just to connect with other community members who can offer education and support on their journey (Cipolletta, Votadoro, & Faccio, 2017; Pinto et al., 2008) but who also use online spaces to explore things like using a new name, deciding what pronouns feel most comfortable, and so on (Cannon et al., 2017).

Online spaces can also offer the unique ability to support those in isolated areas who are struggling with mental health issues. Crisis chat lines, like The Trevor Project, provide a judgment-free space for LGBTQ+ individuals who are under the age of twenty-five. Specifically, the chat line offers LGBTQ+ individuals the ability to talk with someone about issues that may be negatively impacting them and receive support in the form of empathetic listening. The Trevor Project also provides social identity and culture-specific resources through the sharing of online resources that can educate youth, as well as those seeking to help youth, who may be struggling with issues related to gender, sexuality, or mental health. Resources like these are a striking example of how technology has encouraged new methods of fostering strengths and support, as many of the counselors that speak to the youth for the Trevor Project are LGBTQ+ individuals themselves or are allies – individuals who have been touched in some way by a member of the LGBTQ+ community and want to give back to young community members (Goldbach, Rhoades, Green, Fulginiti, & Marshal, 2019).

Moreover, The Trevor Project is consistent with the present stigma and strengths framework. In critical ways, it is unlike traditional crisis lines because it provides empathetic interactions that affirm an individual's identity and provides them with contact with someone who knows about the unique experience they might be going through and can offer support through normalizing language, free of judgment. Because heterosexual and cis-gendered individuals never have to experience the process of "coming out" and the challenges that come with it, such as being in an unsupportive home or community, they do not have the need for this service in the same way that many LGBTQ+ youth do. The Trevor Project is just one of many ways that LGBTQ+ individuals have seen a need within their community due to stigmatization and found a way to provide support through approaches that seek to reduce stigma yet recognize and cultivate strengths.

In addition to nudging individuals to share and connect with one another about their social identities, online spaces also offer a new mode of activism. While some of this activism might include sharing about issues impacting the LGBTQ+ community, it also affords a place where outgroup members can be reached more widely than the marches and other activities of the past could (Shapiro, 2008). Also, online spaces offer accessibility, which may benefit individuals in their ability to become more involved in activism and as a result promote their social well-being (Klar & Kasser, 2009). However, this media can also open the door to new forms of discrimination and bullying against community members, especially when many people are able to make comments and posts anonymously (Green, Bobrowicz, & Siang Ang, 2015).

Thus, when thinking about possible future interventions to promote positive contact and social support for LGBTQ+ individuals, technology and media stand out as critical, timely, and accessible tools to share experiences across groups (Brannon, & Walton, 2013; Drushel, 2010; Fox & Ralston, 2016), it has potential to address social inequalities yet it can also facilitate social disparities (e.g., bullying). Additionally, media might also serve as an efficacious method of conducting ingroup interventions, particularly among ingroup members coming from different race and class experiences. That is, even though LGBTQ+ is an umbrella term, those who come from identities that intersect within multiple stigmatized and marginalized communities often experience higher levels of discrimination (Hughto, Reisner, & Pachankis, 2015; Worthen, 2017). Among those most marginalized within the LGBTQ+ umbrella are African American transgender women who face discrimination within African American spaces, feminist spaces, and LGBTQ+ spaces for their identity and often have a much harder time accessing resources than their White American or cis-gendered peers (Kattari, Walls, Whitfield, & Langenderfer Magruder, 2016).

4.3 Community Support as Strengths: Implications for Mainstream Settings

Young Black/African American transgender women make up a disproportionate number of those at risk in the United States for infection with HIV, with an estimated prevalence of 56 percent (Herbst et al., 2008 Poteat., Malik, Scheim, & Elliott, 2017; Poteat et al., 2019). In much the same way that LGBTQ+ individuals stood together in the 1980s to support one another during the increased isolation and escalated stigmatized status of the HIV/AIDs epidemic in the United States, social support remains key in moderating the psychosocial and structural factors of HIV (Silva et al., 2019). The epidemic in the 1980s brought with it the need to dispel misinformation about the virus, as well as to address structural issues such as a lack of medical care, tasks that were often taken up by other LGBTQ+ individuals. In particular, lesbians who were trained in nursing and general caretaking played an active role in addressing such needs; their actions were often construed as both a means to provide social support and an act of political resistance (Schneider & Stoller, 1995). This resistance and social support were especially important to LGBTQ+ individuals when government at the time was passing policies such as the Helms Amendment in 1987, which made it illegal to use federal funding for HIV prevention projects that may encourage same-sex partnerships (Vaid, 1995).

While there is much to be said about the stigmatization that came with HIV/ AIDs, it is important to also note that these barriers have continued to bring LGBTQ+ individuals together in unique ways, pushing them to develop and implement resources of their own to care for one another. One creative, collective, and adaptive response to come out of the stigmatization of HIV/AIDs is the House and Ball/ballroom subcultures which have been especially popular among Black and Latino gay men (Kubicek, McNeeley, Weiss, & Kipke, 2012). These subcultures continues to be important to the resiliency and strength of these intersectional communities, offering support, acceptance, and entertainment to community members (Wong, Schrager, Holloway, Meyer, & Kipke, 2014). One of the reasons why these groups are called "houses" is that they have traditionally offered the support of a chosen family when many of the individuals involved in them have been ostracized from their biological families (Arnold & Bailey, 2009; Levitt, 2019). Not only in the height of the HIV/AIDS epidemic did LGBTQ+ individuals care for one another, but they continue to do so, in groups like the Ball and House communities, and also in LGBTQ+ centers that can be found across the country, specializing in care that caters to the unique experiences of members of the community (Hudson, 2018) and organizations like the Human Rights Campaign, which continues to fight for rights and access to resources for marginalized LGBTQ+ individuals. Such services provide access to spaces that meet critical needs including health care, mental health resources, housing, and social support in the form of group gatherings, shared knowledge through mentorships, and gender-affirming clothing donations.

Community social support is an important factor in LGBTQ+ adults who are aging with HIV for maintaining their independence and quality of life (Brennan-Ing, Seidel, Larson, & Karpiak, 2013), as well as younger community members who are still developing their individual identity and trying to find a place for themselves among broader groups (Hackimer & Proctor, 2014). Thus, mainstream institutions should strive to implement policies and practices that make it possible and accessible for LGBTQ+ individuals to cultivate and receive social support from ingroup members. Consistent with this implication, research on racial/ethnic minorities supports the importance of polices and practices within mainstream institutions that foster ingroup connections and social support for addressing social disparities. For instance, Brannon and Lin (in press) have shown the specific benefits of engagement with practices that allow Latino/a/x and Black/African American college students to access ingroup sources of support, and even a sense of connection with ingroup members, for several outcomes tied to inequalities including institutional belonging, academic achievement including graduation rates, as well as well-being indicators.

4.4 Motivating Policies and Practices That Minimize Stigma and Identity Concealment

Within mainstream settings, there is a need for policies and practices to minimize stigma and identity concealment among LGBTQ+ individuals. To justify this need, we review some historical practices and consequences tied to stigma and identity concealment. The AIDS epidemic made an individual's choice of identity concealment more difficult for some LGBTQ+ individuals; nonetheless, conceal-ment has continued to be a persistent aspect of everyday life for many others, often resulting in negative mental health effects (Newheiser, Barreto, & Tiemersma, 2017; Rood et al., 2017). In 1972, Allen Young wrote an essay that first touched on the concept of LGBTQ+ individuals leaving (and coining the term) "the closet" as an act of sharing their otherwise concealed identity, (Jay & Young, 1972). The concept of "the closet" remains important as it continues to imply that LGBTQ+ individuals have a choice in whether or not to share their identity, despite the often pathologized stigma attached to that identity. It's critical to note that it wasn't until 1973 that the American Psychological Association (APA) removed homosexuality from the *Diagnostic and Statistical Manual of Mental Disorders* (DSM), and 1975 when the US government lifted the ban on gays and lesbians in civil service. Even now practices like conversion therapy remain legal within a majority of US states; in some, it remains legal to practice conversion therapy on minors.

Conversion therapy pushes the idea that sexuality is a choice and one can be taught not to be gay or transgender through a method of counseling and prayer (Tozer & Hayes, 2004). Though it continues to be legal to practice conversion therapy in many states, many studies have found long-term, damaging mental health effects on those who have participated in this type of therapy, such as a significant increase in lifetime suicide attempts among transgender adults who were exposed to gender identity conversion therapy before the age of ten (Turban, Beckwith, Reisner, & Keuroghlian, 2019). Conversion efforts, by for instance denouncing the importance of social acceptance, also contradict recent research that finds transgender identity affirmation in youth (e.g., providing opportunities for identity support and expression) results in normative and beneficial mental health outcomes when compared to cis-gendered peers

(Olson, Durwood, DeMeules, & McLaughlin, 2016; Russell, Pollitt, Li, & Grossman, 2018).

Another persistent example of policies and practices within mainstream institutions that promote identity concealment among LGBTQ+ individuals involves the US military. It was not until the Don't Ask, Don't Tell Repeal Act of 2010 that lesbian, gay, and bisexual individuals were able to openly serve in the military and not until 2016 that transgender individuals were allowed to openly serve. Research documents that this type of concealment can have meaningful impacts on individuals who are required to conceal an important part of themselves while their straight peers are encouraged to be their whole selves (Baker, 2007). Impact of the Don't Ask, Don't Tell policy included severe mental harm, some irreparable, to many individuals as well as doubling the number of discharges for disorderly conduct during its implementation (Burks, 2011; Marche, 2019).

Though LGB individuals are now allowed to openly serve in the military, a recent ban in 2019 revoked the ability of transgender individuals to do so. These policy changes affect not only the LGBTQ+ members of the military but also the wider population as they send consequential messages that push a narrow construction of masculinity that conforms to a stereotypical view (Alford & Lee, 2016; Courtenay, 2000). While research has not been conducted on the most recent policy change, past studies have looked at the previous transgender ban that showed an impact on both transgender individuals' morale and the morale of members of the transgender community as a whole (Kerrigan, 2012). The sudden exclusion of the transgender individuals from military service sends an explicit message that transgender individual may not be seen as worthy to integrate into a large institution like the military, leaving even those who had no intention of joining the military potentially feeling as though they are a burden on society (Haas, Rodgers, & Herman, 2014; Kerrigan, 2012). Hence, as previously discussed, past studies have looked at the importance of gender recognition and support. These studies highlight the importance for policies and practices within larger institutions to take into account ways to promote inclusive rules and regulations that integrate all members of the LGBTQ+ community (Olson, Durwood, DeMeules, & McLaughlin, 2016; Russell, Pollitt, Li, & Grossman, 2018).

4.5 How Mainstream Institutions Can Leverage "Pride" and Activism

"Pride" as a word and an event is often linked to the LGBTQ+ population in the United States. Through Pride events, many LGBTQ+ individuals have been able to find a sense of acceptance within themselves as they have the opportunity to come together to celebrate their identity and see their identity reflected in others around them, rather than to conceal it. Pride as an event continues to not only be a place and space of social resistance but also serves as a space for the psychological self to combat internalized homophobia through a collective display of identity (Bruce, 2016). Oftentimes Pride within the United States is associated with the month of June, during which many LGBTQ+ individuals celebrate their identity through marches, parades, and other collective events. Although many contemporary and even mainstream representations of Pride conjure images of a party and celebration, it has historically and continues to be a gathering of political resistance against discrimination.

Pride, the event, evolved from marches commemorating the Stonewall Riots, which happened the night of June 27, 1969. While there were many other instances of resistance before the Stonewall riots, one of the reasons this event stands out is that many of the patrons who refused to comply with what had become a ritual of intimidation and arrest by the police at bar spaces were transgender people and people of color, who had a history of being downtrodden. When Allyson Ann Allante, who fought against police in the Stonewall rebellion, was asked if the event was a lesbian and gay or a transgender rebellion, she replied, "both, because it was the first time that both came together to fight off the oppressor and it set a good precedent to do it many times since" (Feinberg, 2005, p. 93). These riots are regarded as one of the first moments in recorded history that exemplify solidarity and the coming together of individuals from diverse and intersectional backgrounds to share a common goal, and in turn developing and fostering strengths and resiliency. Again, Stonewall is a notable example of collective action and resistance in which individuals whose multiple sources of intersecting and marginalized identities placed them at risk for facing the highest levels of discrimination were central and prominent figures.

Pride marches have functioned to allow space for expression and collective gathering; they also have served to encourage individuals to go outside the social norms of general society. With the use of the slogan "out of the bar, into the streets," in reference to Allen Young's 1972 essay (Jay & Young, 1972), it becomes clear that the intention of many LGBTQ+ individuals is to move or expand their message and visibility to society at large, and it signals a desire for broader acceptance, to no longer bear the weight of identity concealment in their day-to-day lives. Such intentions and desires, in part, gave rise to the gay liberation movement in the 1970s. As Guillaume Marche (2019, p. 33, emphasis added) puts it:

> Part of this movement's vitality is due to the fact that it claims that the differences between homosexuality and heterosexuality are neither

insignificant nor unsurmountable. **Its goal is neither to minimize nor to essentialize them**. Likewise, it is neither fully geared toward integration-ism nor separatism: it neither aims to get gays and lesbians accepted as respectable elements of society nor to reinforce identity boundaries based on sexual orientation.

Thus, consistent with a stigma and strengths approach, the foundations of the gay liberation movement sought to humanize LGBTQ+ individuals by allowing their lived experiences to not be rendered invisible or "minimize[d]" or "essentialize[d]" yet to be complex – tied to stigma and strengths as well as similarities and differences with outgroups. The gay liberation movement also drew together identities and related issues that had previously remained separate from one another under a broader umbrella (such as combining gay and lesbian struggles with transgender hardships). It also fostered activism and other forms of collective action linked to positive psychological well-being, which may have been imperative to the LGBTQ+ individuals' mental health in the face of adversity both then and now (Klar & Kassar, 2009).

Though activism has taken on new forms among LGBTQ+ individuals through technology, a large importance for both digital and in-person community spaces, such as pride events, remains (Bartos & Hegarty, 2019). While Pride as an event celebrated by LGBTQ+ individuals has shifted and taken on different meanings over time, it has remained very much a space where traditionally marginalized and stigmatized individuals can explore their complex or whole selves, as well as share that self with others (Bruce, 2016). It also remains an act of resistance to attend these events, as oppression and discrimination actively continue for many members of this community. Rights and protections for LGBTQ+ individuals remain salient in national headlines. Such headlines highlight limitations as well as progress for transgender rights as a 2020 Supreme Court ruling upheld civil protections while policies in other domains tied to accessing resources (e.g., homeless shelters) have been restricted (Cameron, 2020). Pride is a place of community building and social support, which until everyone under the LGBTQ+ umbrella receives equals rights and recognition remains important to both individual and community identity. For all of these reasons, policies and practices that support the continuation of these spaces are critical. Additionally, policies and practices within mainstream institutions can further intervention efforts by making the values enacted within such pride spaces available to LGBTQ+ individuals and into the broader society to decrease prejudice and negative separation between groups (Brassel & Anderson, 2019; Broockman & Kalla, 2018).

Further, intervention efforts within mainstream institutions can be advanced by expanding on social support for LGBTQ+ inclusive diversity practices (see Woodford, Kulick, Garvey, Sinco, & Hong, 2018). Research with racial/ethnic minority members has demonstrated the efficacy of including opportunities to engage with practices and activities tied to racial/ethnic minority membership, which can be a source of pride, within college and university settings for inclusion and other academic and well-being outcomes among Latino/a/x and Black/African American students (Brannon & Lin, 2020). Similarly, areas of both stigma and strengths within mainstream institutions for LGBTQ+ students may include things like "Lavender Graduation," which the Human Rights Campaign's website (https://www.hrc.org/resources/lavender-graduation) describes as follows (emphasis added):

> an annual ceremony conducted on numerous campuses to honor lesbian, gay, bisexual, transgender, queer and ally students and to acknowledge their achievements and contributions to the University. **The Lavender Graduation Ceremony was created by Dr. Ronni Sanlo, a Jewish Lesbian, who was denied the opportunity to attend the graduations of her biological children because of her sexual orientation.** It was through this experience that she came to understand the pain felt by her students.

Lavender Graduation was largely influenced by the special commencements that have been celebrated at colleges and universities for decades highlighting cultural heritages and the importance of interdependence within these communities that contributed to an individual student's achievement of graduating (Brannon et al., 2015). In a similar way, Lavender Graduation recognizes the unique experiences of LGBTQ+ students of all races and ethnicities, highlighting their academic achievements and the support of peers as part of their academic journey. In short, such efforts within mainstream institutions allow social groups that have a long history of enduring oppression and discrimination to express and celebrate their selves in their full complexity.

4.6 Summary: Application of Stigma and Strengths Framework to LGBTQ+ Individuals

Historically, LGBTQ+ individuals have stepped up to support one another, particularly in the face of hardship, when larger, mainstream institutions would not do so. Using a stigma and strengths framework, we suggest that intervention efforts can benefit from leveraging the ways in which LGBTQ+ individuals have created spaces of support and encouragement for one another, as well as endeavored to promote the visibility of their needs and hardships to outgroup members. By allowing LGBTQ+ individuals to feel comfortable sharing about themselves, mainstream institutions can open the door for greater intergroup understanding and support, through the sharing of knowledge about an individuals' identity, culture, and history that may challenge another individuals' prior perceptions (Brannon, 2018; Brannon, & Walton, 2013). We began this section with a quote from Audre Lorde that proclaimed that there is no such thing as a single-issue struggle. Given the multifaceted nature of social struggles, we suggest that one promising way to intervene, to motivate individuals to recognize and feel compelled to resolve such social issues, is through stigma and strengths approaches. Indeed, such approaches reflect and harness the complexity of social identities. In the next section, we explore the potential for applying the stigma and strengths framework to dominant social groups.

5 Making the Invisible Visible: Examining Dominant Group Identities in Context

> I imagine one of the reasons people cling to their hates so stubbornly is because they sense, once hate is gone, they will be forced to deal with pain.
> – James Baldwin, 1955

While dominant identities can be tied to toxic or stigmatized ideas that can have negative ingroup and outgroup consequences, these identities are more than stigma, stereotypes, or toxic ideas – they are also often a valued source of self that shapes motivations and behavior. And, although social identities tied to dominant groups can be a source of ingroup connection and positive affect, pride and relatedly the development of strengths tied to identity among such groups differ in form and function compared to nondominant groups (e.g., racial/ethnic minorities, sexual orientation minorities). As reviewed in the previous sections, pride practices for marginalized groups reflect multiple needs including the necessity of responding to historical and often ongoing experiences of oppression and discrimination. Thus, expressing pride tied to a dominant identity, in contrast to a marginalized identity, serves different and distinct purposes. Importantly, group identity for dominant groups is often not shaped by the experience of pride that is meaningfully connected to and overlapping with the experience of prejudice (e.g., group practices to survive and cope with long-standing experiences of oppression and discrimination, see DiAngelo, 2016).

This section will highlight findings from social and cultural psychology as well as adjacent fields that shed light on how a stigma and strengths framework applies to dominant social groups. First, an analysis of the role of privilege will highlight how dominant group identity can involve juggling both the stigma attached to privilege and the social advantages tied to group membership. This juggling act and its consequences resonate with the quote from James Baldwin that opens this section. Whiteness and masculinity, two dominant social identities, will be analyzed using the stigma and strengths framework. The role of context will be examined to demonstrate how privileged group identity processes within ingroup settings can have impactful consequences on outgroup members. Finally, the section will describe how interventions can leverage complexity tied to dominant social group identities – their links to sometime toxic ideas and beliefs and their association with valued aspects of self that can be leveraged as strengths to address social disparities. Thus, although distinct in meaningful ways from the psychological selves associated with historically low power/status social groups, the selves associated with dominant social groups, we theorize with reviewed evidence, can be leveraged to shape motivations and behaviors in ways that mitigate social disparities.

5.1 The Privilege Paradox

Privilege can be operationalized as the experience of reaping unearned advantages from one's group identity (McIntosh, 1988). It is a hallmark attribute of dominant social groups, such as whites and men, that have historically been at the top of the social hierarchy in Western societies like the United States. As such, privilege is often a group trait that members of dominant groups seek to protect to maintain the status tied to their social identity (Lowery et al., 2006). The drive to maintain group status can lead members of dominant groups to employ defense mechanisms when faced with threats to this status or evidence of their privilege, such as whites refusing to acknowledge the benefits afforded to them by their race/ethnicity and claiming that they experience racial discrimination (Knowles et al., 2014; Phillips & Lowery, 2015). These behaviors contribute to the maintenance of social institutions that reinforce stigma toward outgroups and significant societal inequalities including the gender wage gap (Miller, Taylor, & Buck, 1991) and the racial gap in accumulation of financial capital (Katznelson, 2005).

Members of dominant groups are often motivated to ignore or rationalize the advantages that their group identity grants them because this motivated lack of awareness justifies their inaction to rectify systemic inequalities brought about by privilege and relieves feelings of cognitive dissonance (Jost, Banaji, & Nosek, 2004; Phillips & Lowery, 2018). Thus, dominant group members often perform an intricate cognitive dance wherein they downplay or ignore the advantages afforded to them while benefiting from these same advantages. These characteristics of privilege make increasing allyship within dominant groups a challenging task, yet also an urgent one. Another barrier to cultivating allyship among dominant group members like White Americans is that members of such groups often do not conceptualize themselves as being white but rather see other groups as "having" race (Markus, 2008). As previously noted in the Element, this is a defining feature of privilege: it allows members of dominant groups to view themselves as individuals, whereas social groups that are forced to contend with the burden of discrimination and stereotyping are not granted the same freedom to be individuals and instead are seen through the imposed lens of their gender or racial/ethnic group membership.

Only within the past forty years have researchers begun to study privilege as a psychological phenomenon; however, a growing body of research has mapped out some important ways that privilege shapes behavior. For example, an issue of the *Journal of Social Issues* from 2012 on systems of privilege contains several articles in which researchers examined the effects of raising awareness of privilege (Stewart et al., 2012), used intersectional approaches to explore how privileged group members reinforce the status quo (Ferber, 2012), and investigated interventions to increase allyship behavior (Case et al., 2012). One underexamined domain in research on privilege that several of these articles note as a future direction is the everyday, in-group social interactions that dominant group members have with one another that reinforce and perpetuate the stigmatization of outgroups (see also Phillips & Lowery, 2018). This section will highlight the potential of using a stigma and strengths approach to study dominant groups and develop interventions that increase awareness of privilege and motivate members of dominant groups to reduce social inequities.

5.2 Examining Whiteness and Masculinity as Case Studies in Privileged, Complex Identities

Social identity theory explains how race and gender are fundamental identities and inform a wide range of attitudes and behaviors (Tajfel & Turner, 1986). While race and gender are perhaps the most salient social identities, research on intersectionality has shown that multiple identities can become salient in a given context in complex ways that shape behavior (Crenshaw, 1991). Religion, ideology, social class, immigrant status, and sexual orientation can all have additive and/or complex effects on behavior in different contexts. Crucially, the *intersection* of these identities in a given social context can lead to attitude formation and behavior that would not be uniquely explained by analyzing any single identity in isolation. Intersectionality has provided many insights into the psychological experiences of groups with multiple stigmatized social identities, such as women of color (Crenshaw, 1991; Nash, 2008). Yet, neither white nor masculine identity has been critically evaluated from an intersectional, ingroup process perspective in the social sciences until more recently (see Cole, 2009; Liu, 2017). Understanding the compounding effects of holding multiple dom-inant identities (e.g., white and male) on daily experience including access to privilege may also inform and broaden insights tied to understanding the effects of holding multiple stigmatized identities (e.g., Black and female). For such reasons, whiteness and masculinity, two dominant social identities, deserve theoretical scrutiny; intersectional understandings of such dominant social identities may contribute to insights about group norms that perpetuate racist and sexist attitudes and behaviors (Liu, 2017; Mahalik et al., 1998). Consistent with this potential, we integrate and review research to compare and contrast the privileged natures of these two identities and then examine the nature of the societal context of white male power structures. In so doing, we seek to examine how selves tied to dominant groups perpetuate group inequalities, the social contexts that enable and support these behaviors, and ways to change them.

5.3 White Identity: A Blank Slate?

The scientific literature on white identity has grown significantly in recent years. More psychological articles have been published on white identity in the past ten years than in the previous century. A recent search on the PsycINFO online database for articles with "white identity" in the title or abstract published between 1909 and 2009 returned 2,506 articles, while the same search for articles published between 2010 and 2019 returned 2,807 articles. Sociologists and critical race theorists have done a great deal of work in mapping the broader societal effects of whiteness, creating a theoretical foundation that other social scientists use to study white identity. One such guiding sociological work is *White Fragility: Why It's So Hard for White People to Talk about Racism*, a book by Robin DiAngelo summarizing her years of research on the processes whites employ to maintain their racial superiority (DiAngelo, 2018).

White fragility is defined as the tendency for whites to respond to information about racism or racial privilege with "anger, withdrawal, emotional incapacitation, guilt, argumentation, and cognitive dissonance" (DiAngelo, 2018, p. 55.). This aligns with the psychological literature on how dominant group members respond to threats to their group identity (see Dovidio & Gaertner, 2004; Knowles et al., 2014). Hence, this is one reason why intergroup interactions are associated with anxiety and avoidance; such interactions, especially when involving topics related to discrimination and oppression, can be a source of threat for both dominant and nondominant group members (Bodenhausen & Richeson, 2010; Goff, Steele, & Davies, 2008). In many ways, *White Fragility* is an exposé on privilege – it even includes a section of a chapter titled "White Solidarity" describing it as "the unspoken agreement among whites to protect white advantage" (DiAngelo, 2018, p. 57).

The key word "unspoken" implies that even for the most racially liberal, "woke" (highly aware of social inequalities) whites, there are societal and psychological pressures to avoid confronting racism and turn a blind eye to one's racial privilege. DiAngelo frames white solidarity as one mechanism through which racism is enabled, drawing attention to how whites punish other whites who confront racism (violating norms of ingroup solidarity) and do not punish whites who passively ignore racism (thus acting in line with normative behavior). These norms serve as potent barriers to allyship behavior and, in doing so, tacitly reinforce white supremacy and whites' willful ignorance of their racial privilege. Consequently, whites' lack of exposure to meaningful racial discussion with other whites further serves to perpetuate aversive racism, less blatant yet more subtle forms of prejudice or discrimination (Crandall, Eshleman, & O'Brien, 2002).

This is an important point – that ingroup processes that build solidarity and group cohesion can be predicated on norms and behavior that further stigmatize outgroups, in this case people of color. Empirical research on white privilege has shown that these norms are closely tied to motivations to maintain one's group status (e.g., Phillips & Lowery, 2018), yet the everyday behaviors dictated by these norms have not been empirically scrutinized. Studying pride and belonging behaviors, such as how whites bond with other whites and discuss racialized topics such as immigration policy or policing reform, is crucial to better understand how privilege is enacted in quotidian contexts. Studying these behaviors and group processes from an intersectional approach, one that takes into account the multiple, complex identities that dominant group members hold, will provide insights into potential identity-based interventions that target white privilege. Prior work has shown that it is important to take into account multiple dimensions of intersectionality, such as social class, race, and gender, to avoid misattributing behavior to an individual's single identity rather than the confluence of their intersecting identities (Carbado, 2013).

5.4 Masculinity: A Valued yet Precarious Social Identity

The field of psychology has historically, and still is, largely male dominated (see Gruber et al., in press for discussion of the underrepresentation of women and other social groups within psychological science), which may explain why male ingroup processes have not been studied until quite recently. Research conducted by Valerie Purdie-Greenaway (2018) shows that although women earn 75 percent of psychology PhDs, they represent less than half of all psychology faculty (with gender inequality further increasing as seniority in the career trajectory increases). As discussed previously, members of socially dominant groups – even academics – face normative pressures to avoid critically analyzing any privileges they hold. There has been a plethora of psychological research on the ingroup processes of minority racial groups (e.g., Eberhardt & Fiske, 1998; Bodenhausen & Richeson, 2010) yet only a handful of publications applying this same approach to dominant groups (e.g., Unzueta & Binning, 2012). Exploring the ingroup processes of men will lead to a better understanding of the socialization, normalization, and justifications of male privilege.

Moreover, masculine identity tied to mainstream American ideas and practices shares many psychological characteristics with white identity – both are socially dominant identities that experience distinct privileges. Men and White Americans respond to threat in similar ways, by denying or refusing to acknowledge discrimination to avoid the questioning of their unearned social status (Adams, Tormala, & O'Brien, 2006; Knowles et al., 2014). While it is important to consider the behavior of dominant group members in situations where they perceive their status is being threatened, situations where such individuals are at ease and linked to bonding with one another are also psychologically relevant. An example made salient by President Donald Trump's sexist comments in a 2005 *Access Hollywood* audio recording is the fraternal bonding that takes place in male-dominated spaces (e.g., locker rooms; Fahrenthold, 2016). Studies analyzing the content of speech among college male athletes in locker room and bar settings have found that their conversations can reaffirm traditional masculine norms by dehumanizing women and encouraging sexist behavior (Curry, 1991, 1998). This work demonstrates how outgroup prejudice can be intertwined with the processes of ingroup bonding and status affirmation for dominant groups such as men. In American society, masculine group membership often involves othering women as a means to win status and respect from other men. This is one example of how dominant group practices associated with pride and ingroup connections, such as feeling good about one's manhood and connecting with other men, may result in the stigmatization of outgroups such as women.

Whites may also engage in ingroup favoritism and solidarity behaviors that end up harming racial/ethnic minority outgroups, for instance, by telling racist jokes. The pressure to not confront someone telling a racist joke in an all-white setting can be immense due to the norm of preserving white solidarity (DiAngelo, 2018). For socially dominant groups like men and whites it is possible to casually use prejudiced language and bonding behavior that reinforces group inequalities as a means to bolster their own ingroup belonging and are largely unaware of the consequences of their actions due to their privileged status (Phillips & Lowery, 2018). Additional psychological insights into masculinity and white identity can be gained from focusing on the ingroup processes that dictate the acceptability of this behavior. Specifically, research might focus on how dominant group members experience stigmas tied to their identities (e.g., men repressing emotions, men acting aggressively) and how strengths related to these same identities (e.g., standing up for others, expressing oneself with confidence) can be used to address these stigmas and broader social disparities.

Understanding the shared mechanisms of whiteness and masculinity involves examining the components of these social identities individually in addition to examining how they intersect. For example, are all-white discussions of racial issues influenced by gender? Is all-male discourse on topics of gender influenced by race? What is the role of social class in influencing gender and racial group belonging? Comparing and contrasting whiteness and masculinity has illustrated some of their shared psychological mechanisms, such as the motivation to deny one's privilege being grounded in collective guilt (Branscombe, 2004). This research provides evidence of how motivation to avoid the stigma and negative emotions associated with collective guilt motivate attitudes and behavior among dominant groups.

5.5 Pride, Privilege, and Prejudice within Dominant Groups

Ingroup social interactions, the typical behaviors that members of dominant groups engage in with each other, are ripe for psychological study. These interactions consist of two key psychological components: the everyday behaviors themselves at the individual level (e.g., talking, joking, arguing) and the norms that dictate them at the intuitional level (e.g., avoiding the confrontation of racism). Studying these phenomena from a stigma and strengths perspective could allow researchers to take into account how individuals' privileged and disadvantaged identities may intersect in complex ways. This approach is inspired by Kurt Lewin's model for action research: identifying hard-to-change, problematic behavioral patterns; shifting them in the contexts in which they naturally occur; then establishing new, more beneficial behavioral patterns (Lewin, 1946). Several major problem areas could benefit from research that uses this approach, including better understanding of the blinding effects of privilege, how fragile or robust dominant identities are in the absence (vs. presence) of group status threat, and the social contexts that perpetuate status-legitimizing beliefs.

5.6 Removing the Blinders of Privilege

Mapping the patterns of how members of dominant groups make meaning of and discuss privilege with one another, given their motivations to, sometimes, ignore their own privilege, is an important area for future research to continue exploring. Several research questions in this domain follow: What are the topics that are uncomfortable for dominant groups to discuss? How do dominant group members respond to information showing that privilege is keeping them from addressing important social issues? Can dominant group members, when made aware of their privilege, wield it to successfully reduce group inequities? Past research using the stigma and strengths approach has shown that taking part in activities such as cross-group interactions or academic courses that involve active engagement with cultural ideas and practices associated with racial/ ethnic minority groups can promote dominant group members' support for policies that explicit address social inequalities and benefit outgroup members (Brannon, 2018; Brannon & Walton, 2013; see also Figure 5). Studies that answer the questions posed here will provide valuable insights into interventions that exploit the precarious balancing act of privilege maintenance – benefiting from privilege while actively ignoring it.

Qualitative research has examined awareness of privilege among White American women interested in getting involved in anti-racism work. For instance, Case (2013) coded interviews with White American women and described themes that highlight how privilege shapes perceptions of inequality: When asked to describe themselves, very few women used the term "White," several mentioned difficulty confronting racism due to concerns for their group membership/comfort, and several others noted that they struggled with viewing whiteness as a positive identity because it is so intertwined with racial superiority. The themes highlighted by this study demonstrate the complexity of navigating dominant group identity and also illustrate the need for more studies that empirically test whether positive construals of white identity that frame privilege as a tool to help others can motivate allyship behavior and positive self-image.

Finally, intervention efforts can remove blinders including hidden or "unseen" sources of privilege that have implications for intergroup perceptions and empathy. For example, Stephens, Hamedani, Markus, Bergsieker, and Eloul (2009) collected perspectives of victims and survivors of Hurricane Katrina, including those who evacuated and those who remained in New Orleans. Stephens and colleagues found that the overwhelming majority of individuals who remained in New Orleans during Hurricane Katrina were from working-class backgrounds and had limited access to resources such as a car or income that could have aided potential efforts to evacuate. In samples that included first responders who helped in the aftermath of Hurricane Katrina as well as college students and an adult (non-college student) sample, all from overwhelming middle-class backgrounds, Stephens and colleagues found that perceptions of those who did not evacuate relative to those who did was negative and consistent with victim blaming. Stephens and colleagues present such findings in a models of agency framework that highlights a source of misunderstanding and that has implications for empathy even in an extreme circumstance such as a natural disaster. That is, consistent with other empirical findings within cultural psychology literatures, they conceptualize and find evidence that individuals from working-class and middle-class backgrounds use different models of agency. Specifically, individuals from working-class backgrounds often use a conjoint model of agency, in which good action responds to situations and other individuals, whereas individuals from middle-class backgrounds often use a disjoint model of agency, in which good action involves influencing situations.

Left invisible, unseen, and not revealed, these two models of agency can clash and in the case of Hurricane Katrina can be tied to many individuals from middle-class backgrounds perceiving actions taken by many individuals from working-class backgrounds as negative and worthy of blame (see Brannon et al., 2017). Using this very important empirical and real-world example, a practical implication for intervention efforts involves the significance of making visible what is particular (i.e., non-universal), as invisibility can fuel perceptions of universality and misunderstandings about the selves and related psychological experiences including perceptions of actions tied to dominant groups.

5.7 The Precariousness of Dominant Identities in Privileged Contexts

As described earlier, members of dominant groups typically respond to status-threatening information with defense mechanisms that alleviate this threat rather than attempting to engage and understand it. Knowles and colleagues (2014) describe three typical responses that whites use when confronted with meritocratic or group status threat: *denial* of privilege, *distancing* their self-concepts from the social identity in question, or supporting policies and behaviors that *dismantle* white privilege. While all three responses serve to protect one's sense of self, denial and distancing responses function as defense mechanisms to preserve one's privilege, while dismantle responses focus instead on improving the ingroup's image by supporting actions that reduces the group's privilege. Research should investigate ways to shift such dismantle responses that could help mitigate social inequalities to an expression of dominant group members identity – to make such responses a typical, normative behavior rather than solely a response to threat. Relatedly, researchers should study whether dominant identity is more fragile or more robust in a privileged social context. That is, are dominant group members more comfortable discussing privilege with other dominant group members compared with doing so with disadvantaged groups? Researchers should seek to understand the everyday processes that prevent allyship from being perceived as identity-consistent with a dominant identity (e.g., even when made aware of male privilege, are men motivated to change their behavior?).

Additionally, the role of individual agency, feeling as if one can make a difference, should be studied in the context of dominant group members. Specifically, research should investigate the ways in which holding a dominant group identity can translate into allyship. A qualitative study by Wernick (2012) explored ways to leverage social class privilege to increase engagement with social justice causes, a focus that is especially important given the intersectional nature of social class (Brannon, Higginbotham, & Henderson, 2017). Wernick (2012) found that wealthy individuals responded positively and indicated more support for social justice causes when presented with an aspirational self-construal of privilege – that is, a construal of privilege grounded in critical reflection that focuses on growth and using one's privilege to address social issues. This method of highlighting the negative consequences of privilege to members of dominant groups (stigmas) then modeling how privilege can also be wielded as a tool to help others (strengths) is a promising research direction. Focusing on an ingroup construal of privilege (e.g., what are you and others in your social group doing with your privilege to help others?) may shift group norms and behaviors toward allyship. Emerging research has shown that highlighting harmful aspects of traditional masculinity (e.g., historically prevalent representations of masculinity that are restrictive and tied to exercising dominance) and then modeling a more inclusive masculinity (e.g., increasingly common representations of masculinity that are prosocial and denounce constraints associated with traditional masculinity such as not expressing emotions) can reduce conformity to sexist norms and increase interest in joining a consent-focused organization (Fisher & Brannon, in prep).

5.8 Harnessing Selves Tied to Dominant Groups to Decrease Social Disparities

In the wake of social movements such as Black Lives Matter and #MeToo, the public is increasingly interested in social issues including the critical evaluation of power structures that stem from white and male ingroup processes. This interest is reflected in recent increases in media attention on issues related to dominant group processes, such as men not being able to express emotions to each other (e.g., Jaramillo, 2019) and male overrepresentation in scientific conference panels (Belluck, 2019). This should serve as motivation for social scientists to apply the stigma and strengths framework to the study of these dominant groups with a focus on shared mechanisms: the blinding effects of privilege, the fragility of dominant identities under threat, and contexts where ingroup bonding leads to outgroup discrimination.

Interventions designed to manipulate each of these mechanisms should be developed and tested to find empirically valid ways to encourage dominant group members to engage with and interrogate group processes tied to their social identity that foster social disparities. Research from cultural psychology has shown that sharing cultural practices and traditions associated with negatively stereotyped, racial/ethnic minority groups with dominant groups can improve intergroup attitudes (Brannon & Walton, 2013). Mainstream institutions can facilitate this process by implementing diversity and inclusion initiatives that foster meaningful intergroup contact that satisfies Allport's contact principles and that create opportunities for dominant group members to engage with ideas and practices associated with the cultural backgrounds of non-dominant group members (Allport, 1954; see Figure 5). However, this solution might require a relatively diverse intergroup population and also places some of the burden for raising awareness of privilege on members of minority groups. Additionally, sometimes diversity courses that effectively increase awareness of white privilege and support for affirmative action do not address the ingroup processes that maintain privileged status (Case, 2007, 2013). Thus, interventions are needed to motivate dominant group members to engage with their assumptions and beliefs about stereotyped, non-dominant groups when members of those groups are absent from the immediate social context.

Future research should focus on ways to frame the engagement of dominant groups' privilege in ways that are nonthreatening or that trigger threat in ways that galvanize allyship behavior. One possible frame is self-growth: learning more about oneself by learning how culture has shaped the identities one holds. This frame aligns with prior research on self-complexity showing that thinking about how one defines one's identity can motivate behavior change without triggering a backlash response (Brannon et al., 2018). Another possibility is to trigger group identity threat and then harness that reactance or backlash and direct it toward a productive, privilege-dismantling response instead of the deny and/or distance responses (e.g., "Direct your frustration toward dismantling the power structures that created the inequality that led to this frustration."). Such future directions could help researchers identify social processes that lead to dismantling privilege. These insights could be harnessed to develop interventions to promote those behaviors in the place of existing behaviors that lead to denial/distancing. Crucially, such interventions will need to ensure that the dismantling behavior is aligned with the needs of minority groups rather than an expression of, for example, benevolent sexism (Glick & Fiske, 2018).

Interventions that change norms around toxic behaviors such as bullying have also been shown to be effective at changing behavior throughout large social networks (Paluck, Shepherd, & Aronow, 2016). These methods could be applied to address harmful dominant ingroup processes and reshape dominant group norms around belonging to be more empathic and inclusive of the perspectives of other groups. Paluck and colleagues (2016) used a social network intervention design to successfully shift norms around bullying in fifty-six schools, in turn reducing incidents of bullying. Social network mapping allows for the identification of social referents, individuals within social groups who are connected to many others. Selectively intervening with these social referents has been shown to have "ripple effects" in a network, where the intervention effects from the intervention spread from the referents to the rest of the network via social interactions.

Utilizing methods that make use of social networks can solve a potential roadblock to interventions: often the individuals who need the intervention the most (e.g., endorse the most toxic ideas about privilege and social dominance) are the hardest to reach or the most reluctant to participate in such interventions. Administering an intervention to increase awareness of privileged behaviors and motivate allyship behavior in, for example, a college fraternity, would only need to identify a handful of social referents, administer the intervention to them, and then track behavior for all members of the fraternity to see how the intervention effects spread. Accordingly, a study on modeling inclusive masculinity in a fraternity setting found that after repeated guided discussions about the nature of masculinity and its effects on men and others, the fraternity brothers expressed more positive attitudes toward homosexuals and other outgroups (Anderson, 2008).

5.9 Summary: Application of Stigma and Strengths Framework to Dominant Groups

Members of dominant social groups must choose how to navigate the world with privilege. Group norms and mainstream institutions may reward ignoring privilege, including how it shapes one's experiences, but an aspirational or growth-centered construal of self can lead to taking action to reduce group inequities. This section incorporated theory on the nuances of intersectional identities and social identity processes to advocate for the development of interventions that address privilege in the contexts where it is maintained. Such interventions are not only urgently needed; they are also feasible and hold the potential to directly address persistent social issues that stem from sexist and racist group norms. Studying the social interactions of dominant groups using a stigma and strengths framework could translate into evidence-based curriculum for diversity courses, structure for workshops that advocate for sexual consent, and guidelines for social justice movements to garner support from privileged individuals. The applications of this research could be impactful by, for example, informing efforts to garner support among dominant group members for policy reforms that principally affect nondominant groups, such as police reform or maternity leave.

6 Closing Discussion

Across three social groups that vary along a number of dimensions including their history and access to power/status, we explored and applied a stigma and strengths framework. Specifically, we proposed and reviewed evidence that suggests the benefits for advancing and furthering intervention efforts of taking into account the fuller complexity of social identities associated with (a) racial/ethnic minorities, (b) sexual orientation minorities, and (c) racial/ethnic and gender dominant group members. We highlighted how social identities associated with such groups can be tied to stigma and strengths that can be strategically leveraged within mainstream institutions to impact social disparities. Given defining characteristics of psychological selves including their role in shaping motivation and behavior, we theorized and reviewed evidence that policies and practices that harnessed insights related to both stigma and strengths can contribute to mitigating long-standing social inequalities in recursive and wise ways.

Mirroring the complexities tied to social identities and their consequences, immense variance and diversity exist within the social identities that we explored in this Element. For instance, among racial/ethnic minority groups such as Latino/a/x, Asian Americans, and Black/African Americans in the United States, there is great variance in historical and current identity relevant experiences within mainstream institutions. Similarly, among sexual orientation minority groups, there is differential access to power/status, especially in regard to intersectional identities. For example, Mayor Pete Buttigieg is openly gay and an early Democratic candidate for the US 2020 presidency who occupies social identities that intersect to afford privileges as well as oppression and discrimination (e.g., he is White American, male, and gay). Buttigieg has shared the following about how his social identities afford similarities with racial/

ethnic minorities such as African Americans. He was quoted in the *Washington Post* as saying (Samuels, Stanley-Becker, & Janes, 2019):

> While I do not have the experience of ever having been discriminated against because of the color of my skin, I do have the experience of sometimes feeling like a stranger in my own country, turning on the news and seeing my own rights come up for debate, and seeing my rights expanded by a coalition of people like me and people not at all like me.

Such appeals by Buttigieg have received mixed responses, from offense and vehement disagreement to applause and enthusiastic agreement. The current stigma and strengths framework has the potential to validate both perspectives, as it allows for similarities and differences. Thus, in some ways, the lived experiences of sexual orientation minorities who also have dominant group racial/ethnic or gender identities like Buttigieg are similar and resonate with those of racial/ethnic minorities, even though those experiences can also meaningfully differ.

Inherent in the stigma and strengths framework is recognition of the dynamic nature of stigma and strengths and their consequences for individual members of social groups. That is, the framework and underlying theory recognize that strengths are not necessarily tied to positive consequences and stigma is not necessarily tied to negative consequences. It does not essentialize stigma or strengths. Rather, it recognizes and emphasizes the profound potential within mainstream settings to buffer against stigma and related identity experiences that are linked to adverse consequences and to bolster opportunities to promote strengths and related identity experiences that are associated with advantageous consequences. Recent research highlights that institutional failures to minimize or eliminate stigma can come at a cost to furthering innovation (Hofstra, Kulkarni, Galvez, He, Jurafsky, & McFarland, 2020). Such research reveals that individuals from low power/status groups (e.g., gender and racial/ethnic minorities) can have strengths that they might leverage in creative ways to produce innovation in their work (e.g., dissertations); however, those strengths can be rendered latent, which in turn produces negative outcomes for individuals from low power/status groups (e.g., professional achievement) as well as to broader institutions and fields (e.g., science).

Finally, the current stigma and strengths framework also accounts for the dynamic nature of social disparities and experiences that foster social inequalities. That is, it recognizes that what it means for individuals to feel safe and welcomed within mainstream settings, for example, is not a snapshot that is taken at one point in time; rather, those experiences and interactions are happening over time, across several contexts, and with multiple interaction partners. Stigma and strengths approaches instituted by mainstream institutions are adaptive to such dynamic features. These approaches suggest policies and practices that can prevent negative and adverse experiences as well as incorp orate and cultivate resources that can serve supportive and buffering functions. The current stigma and strengths framework, by conceptualizing social identities in their fuller complexities, suggests intervention solutions that are well suited to tackle complicated and long-standing social disparities.

References

Adams, G., Tormala, T. T., & O'Brien, L. T. (2006). The effect of self-affirmation on perception of racism. *Journal of Experimental Social Psychology*, *42*(5), 616–626. http://doi.org/10.1177/0963721418763931

Alford, B., & Lee, S. J. (2016). Toward complete inclusion: Lesbian, gay, bisexual, and transgender military service members after repeal of Don't Ask, Don't Tell. *Social Work*, *61*(3), 257–265. http://doi.org/10.1093/sw/sww033

Allport, G. W. (1954).The nature of prejudice. Cambridge, MA: Longman Higher Education.

Altschul, I., Oyserman, D., & Bybee, D. (2006). Racial-Ethnic Identity in Mid-Adolescence: Content and Change as Predictors of Academic Achievement. Child Development, 77(5), 1155–1169. https://doi.org/10.1111/j.1467-8624.2006.00926.x

American Psychological Association, Boys and Men Guidelines Group. (2018). APA guidelines for psychological practice with boys and men. Retrieved from www.apa.org/about/policy/psychological-practice-boys-men-guidelines.pdf

Anderson, E. (2008). Inclusive masculinity in a fraternal setting. *Men and Masculinities*, *10*(5), 604–620. http://doi.org/10.1177/1097184X06291907

Angelou, M. (1978). *And Still I Rise: A Book of Poems*. Random House.

Arnold, E. A., & Bailey, M. M. (2009). Constructing home and family: How the ballroom community supports African American GLBTQ youth in the face of HIV/AIDS. *Journal of Gay & Lesbian Social Services*, *21*(2–3), 171–188. http://doi.org/10.1080/10538720902772006

Ashkenas, J., Park, H., & Pearce, A. (2017). Even with affirmative action, Blacks and Hispanics are more underrepresented at top colleges than 35 years ago. New York Times, 1–18. Retrieved from https://www.nytimes.com/interactive/2017/08/24/us/affirmative-action.html

Baker, S. (2007). Telling: Living with "Don't Ask, Don't Tell." *Journal of Legal Education*, *57*(2), 187–194. Retrieved from www.jstor.org/stable/42894019

Baldwin, J. (1984). Notes of a native son (Vol. 39). Beacon Press. Boston, MA

Bartoş, S. E., & Hegarty, P. (2019). Negotiating theory when doing practice: A systematic review of qualitative research on interventions to reduce homophobia. *Journal of Homosexuality,* *66*(9), 1262–1286. https://doi.org/10.1080/00918369.2018.1500780

Becerra-Culqui, T. A., Liu, Y., Nash, R., Cromwell, L., Flanders, W. D., Getahun, D., Giammattei, S. V., Hunkeler, E. M., Lash, T. L., Millman, A., Quinn, V. P., Robinson, B., Roblin, D., Sandberg, D. E., Silverberg, M. J., Tangpricha, V., & Goodman, M. (2018). Mental Health of Transgender and Gender Nonconforming Youth Compared With Their Peers. Pediatrics, 141(5), e20173845. https://doi.org/10.1542/peds.2017-3845

Bell, E. L. (1990). The bicultural life experience of career-oriented black women.*Journal of Organizational Behavior, 11*(6), 459–477. http://doi .org/10.1002/job.4030110607

Belluck, P. (2019, June 12). N.I.H. head calls for end to all-male panels of scientists. *New York Times*. Retrieved from www.nytimes.com/2019/06/ 12/health/collins-male-science-panels.html

Benner, A. D., & Graham, S. (2011). Latino adolescents' experiences of discrimination across the first 2 years of high school: Correlates and influences on educational outcomes. *Child Development, 82*(2), 508–519. http://doi.org/10.1111/j.1467-8624.2010.01524.x

Bockting, W. O., Miner, M. H., Romine, R. E. S., Hamilton, A., & Coleman, E. (2013). Stigma, mental health, and resilience in an online sample of the US transgender population. *American Journal of Public Health, 103*(5), 943–951. http://doi.org/10.2105/ajph.2013.301241

Bodenhausen, G. V., & Richeson, J. A. (2010). Prejudice, stereotyping, and discrimination. In R. F. Baumeister & E. J. Finkel (Eds.), *Advanced social psychology: The state of the science*, pp. 341–383. New York: Oxford University Press.

Bonam, C. M., Nair Das, V., Coleman, B. R., & Salter, P. (2019). Ignoring history, denying racism: Mounting evidence for the Marley hypothesis and epistemologies of ignorance. *Social Psychological and Personality Science, 10*(2), 257–265. http://doi.org/10.1177/1948550617751583

Boykin, A. W., Jagers, R. J., Ellison, C. M., & Albury, A. (1997). Communalism: Conceptualization and measurement of an Afrocultural social orientation. *Journal of Black Studies, 27*(3), 409–418. http://doi .org/10.1177/002193479702700308

Brannon, T. N. (2018). Reaffirming King's vision: The power of participation in inclusive diversity efforts to benefit intergroup outcomes. *Journal of Social Issues, 74*(2), 355–376. Special Issue: Commemorating 50th anniversary of Dr. King's speech to behavioral scientists, American Psychological Association. http://doi.org/10.1111/josi.12273

Brannon, T. N., Carter, E. R., Murdock-Perriera, L. A., & Higginbotham, G. D. (2018). From backlash to inclusion for all: Instituting diversity efforts to maximize benefits across group lines. *Social Issues and Policy Review, 12*

(1), 57–90. http://doi.org/10.1111/sipr.12040 Brannon, T. N., Higginbotham, G. D., & Henderson, K. (2017). Class advantages and disadvantages are not so black and white: Intersectionality impacts rank and selves. *Current Opinion in Psychology, 18*, 117–122. http://doi.org/10.1016/j.copsyc.2017.08.029

Brannon, T. N., & Lin, A. (2020, August 10). "Pride and Prejudice" Pathways to Belonging:Implications for Inclusive Diversity Practices Within Mainstream Institutions. AmericanPsychologist. Advance online publication. http://dx.doi.org/10.1037/amp0000643

Brannon, T. N., Markus, H. R., & Taylor, V. J. (2015). "Two souls, two thoughts," two self-schemas: Double consciousness can have positive academic consequences for African Americans. *Journal of Personality and Social Psychology, 108*(4), 586–609. http://doi.org/10.1037/a0038992

Brannon, T. N., Taylor, V. J., Higginbotham, G. D., & Henderson, K. (2017). Selves in contact: How integrating perspectives on sociocultural selves and intergroup contact can inform theory and application on reducing inequality. *Social and Personality Psychology Compass, 11*(7), 1–15. http://doi.org/10.1111/spc3.12326

Branscombe, N. R. (1998). Thinking about one's gender group's privileges or disadvantages: Consequences for well-being in women and men. *British Journal of Social Psychology, 37*(2), 167–184. http://doi.org/10.1111/j .2044-8309.1998.tb01163.x

(2004). A social psychological process perspective on collective guilt. In N. R. Branscombe & B. Doosje (Eds.), *Collective guilt: International perspectives* (pp. 320–334). New York: Cambridge University Press. http://doi.org/10.1093/acprof:oso/9780199659180.003.0017

Brassel, S. T., & Anderson, V. N. (2019). Who thinks outside the gender box? Feminism, gender self-esteem, and attitudes toward trans people. *Sex Roles, 82*, 447–462 http://doi.org/10.1007/s11199-019-01066-4

Brennan-Ing, M., Seidel, L., Larson, B., & Karpiak, S. E. (2013). Social care networks and older LGBT adults: Challenges for the future. *Journal of Homosexuality, 61*(1), 21–52. http://doi.org/10.1080/00918369 .2013.835235

Bronski, M. (2011). A queer history of the United States. Boston: Beacon Press.

Broockman, D., & Kalla, J. (2016). Durably reducing transphobia: A field experiment on door-to-door canvassing. *Science, 352*(6282), 220–224. http://doi.org/10.1126/science.aad9713

Bruce, K. M. F. (2016). *Pride parades: How a parade changed the world.* New York: New York University Press.

Bryan, C. J., Walton, G. M., Rogers, T., & Dweck, C. S. (2011). Motivating voter turnout by invoking the self. *Proceedings of the National Academy of*

Sciences, 108(31), 12653–12656. http://doi.org/10.1073/pnas .1103343108

Burks, D. J. (2011). Lesbian, gay, and bisexual victimization in the military: An unintended consequence of "Don't Ask, Don't Tell"? *American Psychologist, 66*(7), 604–613. http://doi.org/10.1037/a0024609

Cameron, C. (2020, July 24). Trump presses limits on transgender rights over supreme court ruling. New York Times. Retrieved from https://www .nytimes.com

Cannon, Y., Speedlin, S., Avera, J., Robertson, D., Ingram, M., & Prado, A. (2017). Transition, connection, disconnection, and social media: Examining the digital lived experiences of transgender individuals. *Journal of LGBT Issues in Counseling, 11*(2), 68–87. http://doi.org/10 .1080/15538605.2017.1310006

Carbado, D. W. (2013). Colorblind intersectionality. Signs: Journal of Women in Culture and Society, 38(4), 811–845.

Case, K. A. (2007). Raising white privilege awareness and reducing racial prejudice: Assessing diversity course effectiveness. *Teaching of Psychology, 34*(4), 231–235. http://doi.org/10.1080/00986280701700250

(Ed.). (2013). *Deconstructing privilege: Teaching and learning as allies in the classroom.* New York, NY Routledge.

Case, K. A., Iuzzini, J., & Hopkins, M. (2012). Systems of privilege: Intersections, awareness, and applications. *Journal of Social Issues, 68* (1), 1–10. http://doi.org/10.1111/j.15404560.2011.01732.x

Caughy, M. O. B., O'Campo, P. J., Randolph, S. M., & Nickerson, K. (2002). The influence of racial socialization practices on the cognitive and behavioral competence of African American preschoolers. Child Development, 73(5), 1611–1625. https://doi.org/10.1111/1467-8624.00493

Cavalcante, A. (2018). Tumbling into queer utopias and vortexes: Experiences of LGBTQ social media users on Tumblr. *Journal of Homosexuality, 66* (12), 1715–1735. http://doi.org/10.1080/00918369.2018.1511131

Chaney, K. E., & Sanchez, D. T. (2017). Gender-inclusive bathrooms signal fairness across identity dimensions. *Social Psychological and Personality Science, 9*(2), 245–253. http://doi.org/10.1177/1948550617737601

Charles, R., & Ritz, D. (2004). *Brother Ray: Ray Charles' own story.* Cambridge, MA: Da Capo Press.

Chavous, T. M. (2000). The relationships among racial identity, perceived ethnic fit, and organizational involvement for African American students at a predominantly White university. Journal of Black Psychology, 26(1), 79–100. https://doi.org/10.1177/0095798400026001005

Cipolletta, S., Votadoro, R., & Faccio, E. (2017). Online support for transgender people: An analysis of forums and social networks. *Health & Social Care in the Community, 25*(5), 1542–1551. http://doi.org/10.1111/hsc.12448

Cokley, K. O., & Chapman, C. (2008). The roles of ethnic identity, anti-White attitudes, and academic self-concept in African American student achievement. Social Psychology of Education: An International Journal, 11(4), 349–365. https://doi.org/10.1007/s11218-008-9060-4

Cole, E. R. (2009). Intersectionality and research in psychology. *American Psychologist*, 64, 170–180. http://doi.org/10.1037/a0014564

Coulter, R. W. S., Kenst, K. S., Bowen, D. J., & Scout, P. (2014). Research funded by the National Institutes of Health on the Health of Lesbian, Gay, Bisexual, and Transgender Populations. *American Journal of Public Health, 104*(2), e105–112. http://doi.org/10.2105/ajph.2013.301501

Courtenay, W. H. (2000). Constructions of masculinity and their influence on men's well-being: A theory of gender and health. *Social Science & Medicine, 50*(10), 1385–1401. http://doi.org/10.1016/S0277-9536(99) 00390-1

Crandall, C. S., Eshleman, A., & O'Brien, L. (2002). Social norms and the expression and suppression of prejudice: The struggle for internalization. *Journal of Personality and Social Psychology, 82*(3), 359–378. http://doi .org/10.1037/0022-3514.82.3.359

Crenshaw, K. (1991). Mapping the Margins: Intersectionality, Identity Politics, and Violence against Women of Color. Stanford Law Review, 43(6), 1241–1299.

Crocker, J., & Major, B. (1989). Social stigma and self-esteem: The self-protective properties of stigma. *Psychological Review, 96*(4), 608–630. http://doi.org/10.1037/0033-295X.96.4.608

Curry, T. J. (1991). Fraternal bonding in the locker room: A profeminist analysis of talk about competition and women. *Sociology of Sport Journal, 8*(2), 119–135.

  (1998). Beyond the locker room: Campus bars and college athletes. *Sociology of Sport Journal*, 15(3), 205–215. http://doi.org/10.1123/ssj .15.3.205

Davis, L. K., Schneider, B. E., Stoller, N. E., & Patton, C. (1997). Women resisting AIDS: Feminist strategies of empowerment. *Contemporary Sociology, 26*(1), 113. http://doi.org/10.2307/2076643

Degner, J., & Dalege, J. (2013). The apple does not fall far from the tree, or does it? A meta-analysis of parent-child similarity in intergroup attitudes. *Psychological Bulletin, 139*(6), 1270–1304. http://doi.org/10.1037 /a0031436

Dehaan, S., Kuper, L. E., Magee, J. C., Bigelow, L., & Mustanski, B. S. (2013). The interplay between online and offline explorations of identity, relationships, and sex: A mixed-methods study with LGBT youth. *Journal of Sex Research*, *50*(5), 421–434. http://doi.org/10.1080/00224499.2012.661489

DiAngelo, R. (2011). White fragility. *International Journal of Critical Pedagogy*, *3*(3), 54–70.

DiAngelo, R. (2018). *White fragility: Why it's so hard for white people to talk about racism*. Boston, MA: Beacon Press

(2016). What does it mean to be white?: Developing white racial literacy. New York, NY Peter Lang.

Dixon, J., Levine, M., Reicher, S., & Durrheim, K. (2012). Beyond prejudice: Are negative evaluations the problem and is getting us to like one another more the solution? *Behavioral and Brain Sciences*, *35*(6), 411–425. http:// doi.org/10.1017/S0140525X11002214

Douglass, R. P., Conlin, S. E., & Duffy, R. D. (2020). Beyond Happiness: Minority Stress and Life Meaning Among LGB Individuals. *Journal of Homosexuality*, *67*(11), 1587–1602. http://doi.org/10.1080/00918369 .2019.1600900

Dovidio, J. F., & Fiske, S. T. (2012). Under the radar: How unexamined biases in decision- making processes in clinical interactions can contribute to health care disparities. *American Journal of Public Health*, *102*(5), 945–952. http://doi.org/10.2105/AJPH.2011.300601

Dovidio, J. F., & Gaertner, S. L. (2004). Aversive racism. *Advances in Experimental Social Psychology*, *36*, 4–56.

Droogendyk, L., Wright, S. C., Lubensky, M., & Louis, W. R. (2016). Acting in solidarity: Cross-group contact between disadvantaged group members and advantaged group allies. *Journal of Social Issues*, *72*(2), 315–334. http://doi.org/10.1111/josi.12168

Drushel, B. E. (2010). Virtually supportive: Self-disclosure of minority sexualities through online social networking sites. (pp. 76–86) In C. Pullen & M. Cooper, Eds., *LGBT identity and online new media*. London: Routledge.

Dubois, W. E. B. (1903). The souls of Black folk. Chicago, IL: A. C. McClurg and Company.

Eberhardt, J. L., & Fiske, S. T. (Eds.). (1998). *Confronting racism: The problem and the response*. Thousand Oaks, CA. Sage Publications.

Ethier, K. A., & Deaux, K. (1994). Negotiating social identity when contexts change: Maintaining identification and responding to threat. Journal of Personality and Social Psychology, 67(2), 243–251. https://doi.org/ 10.1037/0022-3514.67.2.243

Fahrenthold, D. A. (2016). Trump recorded having extremely lewd conversation about women in 2005. *The Washington Post*. Retrieved from https://www.washingtonpost.com/politics/trump-recorded-having-extremely-lewd-conversation-about-women-in-2005/2016/10/07/3b9ce776-8cb4-11e6-bf8a-3d26847eeed4_story.html

Feinberg, L. (2005). *Transgender warriors: Making history from Joan of Arc to Dennis Rodman*. Boston, MA: Beacon Press.

Ferber, A. L. (2012). The culture of privilege: Color-blindness, post-feminism and Christonormativity. *Journal of Social Issues*, 68, 63–77. http://doi.org/10.1111/j.1540-4560.2011.01736.x

Fink, M., & Miller, Q. (2013). Trans media noments. *Television & New Media*, 15(7), 611–626. http://doi.org/10.1177/1527476413505002

Fisher, P. H., & Brannon, T. N. (in prep). Expanding the definition of masculinity: Interventions to shift sexist attitudes and increase allyship behaviors.

Fox, J., & Ralston, R. (2016). Queer identity online: Informal learning and teaching experiences of LGBTQ individuals on social media. *Computers in Human Behavior*, 65, 635–642. http://doi.org/10.1016/j.chb.2016.06.009

Fryberg, S. A., & Eason, A. E. (2017). Making the invisible visible: Acts of commission and omission. *Current Directions in Psychological Science*, 26(6), 554–559. http://doi.org/10.1177/0963721417720959

Fuligni, A. J., Witkow, M., & Garcia, C. (2005). Ethnic Identity and the Academic Adjustment of Adolescents From Mexican, Chinese, and European Backgrounds. Developmental Psychology, 41(5), 799–811. https://doi.org/10.1037/0012-1649.41.5.799

Gibbons, F., Gerrard, M., Cleveland, M., Wills, T., & Brody, G. (2004). Discrimination and substance use in African American parents and their children. *Journal of Personality and Social Psychology*, 86(4), 517–529. http://doi.org/10.1037/0022-3514.86.4.517

Gleason, H. A., Livingston, N. A., Peters, M. M., Oost, K. M., Reely, E., & Cochran, B. N. (2016). Effects of state nondiscrimination laws on transgender and gender-nonconforming individuals perceived community stigma and mental health. *Journal of Gay & Lesbian Mental Health*, 20 (4), 350–362. http://doi.org/10.1080/19359705.2016.1207582

Glick, P., & Fiske, S. T. (2018). The ambivalent sexism inventory: Differentiating hostile and benevolent sexism. In *Social Cognition* (pp. 116–160). Editor: Susan T. Fiske. City of publication: New York, NY. Routledge. http://doi.org/10.1177/0361684311414832

Goff, P. A., Steele, C. M., & Davies, P. G. (2008). The space between us: Stereotype threat and distance in interracial contexts. *Journal of*

Personality and Social Psychology, 94(1), 91–107. http://doi.org/10.1037 /0022-3514.94.1.91

Goffman, E. (2009). *Stigma: Notes on the management of spoiled identity.* New York: Simon and Schuster.

Goldbach, J. T., Rhoades, H., Green, D., Fulginiti, A., & Marshal, M. P. (2019). Is there a need for LGBT-specific suicide crisis services? *Crisis, 40*(3), 203–208. http://doi.org/10.1027/0227-5910/a000542

Gomillion, S. C., & Giuliano, T. A. (2011). The influence of media role models on gay, lesbian, and bisexual identity. *Journal of Homosexuality, 58*(3), 330–354. http://doi.org/10.1080/00918369.2011.546729

Graf, N., Brown, A., & Patten, E. (2018, April 9). *The narrowing, but persistent, gender gap in pay.* Washington, DC: Pew Research Center.

Green, M., Bobrowicz, A., & Ang, C. S. (2015). The lesbian, gay, bisexual and transgender community online: discussions of bullying and self-disclosure in YouTube videos. Behaviour & Information Technology, 34(7), 704–712. https://doi.org/10.1080/0144929X.2015.1012649

Griffith, K. H., & Hebl, M. R. (2002). The disclosure dilemma for gay men and lesbians: "Coming out" at work. *Journal of Applied Psychology, 87*(6), 1191–1199. http://doi.org/10.1037//0021-9010.87.6.1191

Gruber, J., Mendle, J., Lindquist, K., Schmader, T., Clark, L. A., Bliss-Moreau, E., Akinola, M., Atlas, L., M. Barch, D. M., Barrett, L. F., Borelli, J., Brannon, T., Bunge, S., Campos, B., Cantlon, J., Carter, R., Carter-Sowell, A., Chen, S., Craske, M., Crum, A., Cuddy, A. J.,… Williams, L. A. (in press). The future of women in psychological science. Perspectives in Psychological Science.

Gülgöz, S., Glazier, J. J., Enright, E. A., Alonso, D. J., Durwood, L. J., Fast, A. A., … Olson, K. R. (2019). Similarity in transgender and cisgender children's gender development. *Proceedings of the National Academy of Sciences, 116*(49), 24480–24485. http://doi.org/10.1073 /pnas.1909367116

Haas, A. P., Rodgers, P. L., & Herman, J. L. (2014). *Suicide attempts among transgender and gender non-conforming adults.* Los Angeles, CA: The Williams Institute, pp. 50, 59.

Hackimer, L., & Proctor, S. L. (2014). Considering the community influence for lesbian, gay, bisexual, and transgender youth. *Journal of Youth Studies, 18* (3), 277–290. http://doi.org/10.1080/13676261.2014.944114

Henkel, K. E., Dovidio, J. F., & Gaertner, S. L. (2006). Institutional discrimination, individual racism, and Hurricane Katrina. *Analyses of Social Issues and Public Policy, 6*(1), 99-124. http://doi.org/10.1111/j.1530-2415 .2006.00106.x

Herbst, J. H., Jacobs, E. D., Finlayson, T. J., Mckleroy, V. S., Neumann, M. S., & Crepaz, N. (2007). Estimating HIV prevalence and risk behaviors of transgender persons in the United States: A systematic review. *AIDS and Behavior*, *12*(1), 1–17. http://doi.org/10.1007/s10461-007-9299-3

Hobbs, A. (2014). *A chosen exile*. Cambridge, MA: Harvard University Press.

Hofstra, B., Kulkarni, V. V., Galvez, S. M. N., He, B., Jurafsky, D., & McFarland, D. A. (2020). The diversity–innovation paradox in science. *Proceedings of the National Academy of Sciences*. http://doi.org/10.1073/pnas.1915378117

Holloway, J. E. (Ed.). (2005). Africanisms in American culture. Bloomington: Indiana University Press.

Hudson, K. D. (2018). Identity-conscious services for diverse patients: A descriptive analysis of lesbian, gay, bisexual, and transgender-focused federally qualified community health centers. *Journal of Gay & Lesbian Social Services*, *30*(3), 282–298. http://doi.org/10.1080/10538720.2018.1478353

Hughes, D., Rodriguez, J., Smith, E. P., Johnson, D. J., Stevenson, H. C., & Spicer, P. (2006). Parents' ethnic-racial socialization practices: A review of research and directions for Future study. *Developmental Psychology*, *42*(5), 747–770. http://doi.org/10.1037/0012-1649.42.5.747

Hughto, J. M. W., Reisner, S. L., & Pachankis, J. E. (2015). Transgender stigma and health: A critical review of stigma determinants, mechanisms, and interventions. *Social Science & Medicine*, *147*, 222–231. http://doi.org/10.1016/j.socscimed.2015.11.010

Jackson, S. D. (2017). "Connection is the antidote": Psychological distress, emotional processing, and virtual community building among LGBTQ students after the Orlando shooting. *Psychology of Sexual Orientation and Gender Diversity*, *4*(2), 160–168. http://doi.org/10.1037/sgd0000229

Jaramillo, R. F. (2019, May 10). Why can't men say "I love you" to each other? *New York Times*. Retrieved from https://www.nytimes.com/2019/05/10/style/modern-love-college-i-love-you-man-.html

Jay, K., & Young, A. (1972). Out of the closets: Voices of gay liberation. New York, NY: New York University Press.

Jenzen, O. (2017). Trans youth and social media: Moving between counter-publics and the wider web. *Gender, Place & Culture*, *24*(11), 1626–1641. http://doi.org/10.1080/0966369x.2017.1396204

Johnson, S. E., Richeson, J. A., & Finkel, E. J. (2011). Middle class and marginal? Socioeconomic status, stigma, and self-regulation at an elite university. *Journal of Personality and Social Psychology, 100*(5), 838–852. http://doi.org/10.1037/a0021956

Jones, J. M. (2003). TRIOS: A psychological theory of the African legacy in American culture. *Journal of Social Issues, 59*(1), 217–242.

Jones, K. N., & Brewster, M. E. (2017). From awareness to action: Examining predictors of lesbian, gay, bisexual, and transgender (LGBT) activism for heterosexual people. *American Journal of Orthopsychiatry, 87*(6), 680–689. http://doi.org/10.1037/ort0000219

Jost, J. T., Banaji, M. R., & Nosek, B. A. (2004). A decade of system justification theory: Accumulated evidence of conscious and unconscious bolstering of the status quo. *Political Psychology, 25*(6), 881–919. http://doi.org/10.1111/j.1467-9221.2004.00402.x

Kattari, S. K., Walls, N. E., Whitfield, D. L., & Magruder, L. L. (2016). Racial and ethnic differences in experiences of discrimination in accessing social services among transgender/gender-nonconforming people. *Journal of Ethnic & Cultural Diversity in Social Work, 26*(3), 217–235. http://doi.org/10.1080/15313204.2016.1242102

Katznelson, I. (2005). *When affirmative action was white: An untold history of racial inequality in twentieth-century America.* New York: W.W. Norton & Company.

Kerrigan, M. F. (2012). Transgender discrimination in the military: The new don't ask, don't tell. *Psychology, Public Policy, and Law, 18*(3), 500–518. http://doi.org/10.1037/a0025771

Kiang, L., Yip, T., Gonzales-Backen, M., Witkow, M., & Fuligni, A. J. (2006). Ethnic identity and the daily psychological well-being of adolescents from Mexican and Chinese backgrounds. *Child Development, 77*(5), 1338–1350. http://doi.org/10.1111/j.1467-8624.2006.00938.x

Klar, M., & Kasser, T. (2009). Some benefits of being an activist: Measuring activism and its role in psychological well-being. *Political Psychology, 30*(5), 755–777. http://doi.org/10.1111/j.1467-9221.2009.00724.x

Knowles, E. D., Lowery, B. S., Chow, R. M., & Unzueta, M. M. (2014). Deny, distance, or dismantle? How white Americans manage a privileged identity. *Perspectives on Psychological Science, 9*, 594–609. http://doi.org/10.1177/1745691614554658

Kraus, M. W., Piff, P. K., & Keltner, D. (2011). Social class as culture: The convergence of resources and rank in the social realm. *Current Directions in Psychological Science, 20*(4), 246–250. http://doi.org/10.1177/0963721411414654

Kubicek, K., Mcneeley, M., Holloway, I. W., Weiss, G., & Kipke, M. D. (2012). "It's like our own little world": Resilience as a factor in participating in the Ballroom community subculture. *AIDS and Behavior, 17*(4), 1524–1539. http://doi.org/10.1007/s10461-012-0205-2

Lee, J. (2002). Racial and ethnic achievement gap trends: Reversing the progress toward equity? *Educational Researcher, 31*(1), 3–12. http://doi.org /10.3102/0013189X031001003

Levine, C. S., Markus, H. R., Austin, M. K., Chen, E., & Miller, G. E. (2019). Students of color show health advantages when they attend schools that emphasize the value of diversity. *Proceedings of the National Academy of Sciences, 116*(13), 6013–6018. http://doi.org/10.1073/pnas .1812068116

Levy, D. J., Heissel, J. A., Richeson, J. A., & Adam, E. K. (2016). Psychological and biological responses to race-based social stress as pathways to disparities in educational outcomes. *American Psychologist, 71*(6), 455–473. http://doi.org/10.1037/a0040322

Levitt, H. M. (2019). A psychosocial genealogy of LGBTQ+ gender: An empirically based theory of gender and gender identity cultures. *Psychology of Women Quarterly, 43*(3), 275–297. http://doi.org/10.1177 /0361684319834641

Lewin, K. (1946). Action research and minority problems. *Journal of Social Issues, 2*(4), 34–46. http://doi.org/10.1111/j.1540-4560.1946.tb02295.x

Li, M. (2019). Priming mediated vicarious intergroup contact: How narrative focus influences attitude changes toward gay people, same-sex family, and social dominance. *Imagination, Cognition and Personality, 39*(2), 151–174. http://doi.org/10.1177/0276236618810203

Liu, W. M. (2017). White male power and privilege: The relationship between White supremacy and social class. *Journal of Counseling Psychology, 64* (4), 349. http://doi.org/10.1037/cou0000227

Lorde, A. (1982, February). *Malcolm X weekend.* Retrieved from www .blackpast.org/african-american-history/1982-audre-lorde-learning-60s/

Lowery, B. S., Unzueta, M. M., Knowles, E. D., & Goff, P. A. (2006). Concern for the in-group and opposition to affirmative action. *Journal of Personality and Social Psychology, 90*(6), 961. http://doi.org/10.1037 /0022-3514.90.6.961

Lyness, K. S., & Grotto, A. R. (2018). Women and leadership in the United States: Are we closing the gender gap? *Annual Review of Organizational Psychology and Organizational Behavior, 5*, 227–265. http://doi.org/10 .1146/annurev-orgpsych-032117-104739

Lytle, A., & Levy, S. R. (2015). Reducing heterosexuals' prejudice toward gay men and lesbian women via an induced cross-orientation friendship. *Psychology of Sexual Orientation and Gender Diversity, 2*(4), 447–455. http://doi.org/10.1037/sgd0000135

Mahalik, J. R., Cournoyer, R. J., DeFranc, W., Cherry, M., & Napolitano, J. M. (1998). Men's gender role conflict and use of psychological defenses. *Journal of Counseling Psychology, 45*(3), 247. http://doi.org/10.1037/0022-0167.45.3.247

Major, B., & O'Brien, L. T. (2005). The social psychology of stigma. *Annual Review of Psychology, 56*, 393–421. http://doi.org/10.1146/annurev.psych.56.091103.070137

Marche, G. (2019). *Sexuality, subjectivity, and LGBTQ militancy in the United States.* Amsterdam: University of Amsterdam Press, pp. 25–56. http://doi.org/10.2307/j.ctvkjb3qs.6

Markus, H. R. (2008). Pride, prejudice, and ambivalence: Toward a unified theory of race and ethnicity. *The American Psychologist, 63*(8), 651–670. http://doi.org/10.1037/0003-066X.63.8.651

   (2017). American = independent? *Perspectives on Psychological Science, 12* (5), 855–866. http://doi.org/10.1177/1745691617718799

Markus, H.R., & Moya, P. (Eds.). (2010).Doing race: 21 essays forthe 21st century.New York: W.W. Norton.

Mbiti, J. S. (1970). *African religions and philosophy.* New York: Doubleday.

McCluney, C. L., Robotham, K., Lee, S., Smith, R., & Durkee, M. (2019, November 15). The cost of code-switching. *Harvard Business Review.* Retrieved from https://hbr.org/2019/11/the-costs-of-codeswitching

Mcinroy, L. B., & Craig, S. L. (2015). Transgender representation in offline and online media: LGBTQ youth perspectives. *Journal of Human Behavior in the Social Environment, 25*(6), 606–617. http://doi.org/10.1080/10911359.2014.995392

McIntosh, P. (1988). White privilege: Unpacking the invisible knapsack. In P. S. Rothenberg (Ed.), *Race, class, and gender in the United States: An integrated study* (6th ed. pp. 188–192). New York: Worth

Mendoza-Denton, R., Downey, G., Purdie, V. J., Davis, A., & Pietrzak, J. (2002). Sensitivity to status-based rejection: Implications for African American students' college experience. *Journal of Personality and Social Psychology, 83*(4), 896–918. http://doi.org/10.1037/0022-3514.83.4.896

Meyer, I. H., & Northridge, M. E. (Eds.). (2007). *The health of sexual minorities: Public health perspectives on lesbian, gay, bisexual and transgender populations*. Springer, Boston, MA Springer Science & Business Media. https://doi.org/10.1007/978-0-387-31334-4

Miller, D. T., Taylor, B., & Buck, M. L. (1991). Gender gaps: Who needs to be explained? *Journal of Personality and Social Psychology*, 61(1), 5. http://doi.org/10.1037/0022-3514.61.1.5

Moleiro, C., & Pinto, N. (2015). Sexual orientation and gender identity: review of concepts, controversies and their relation to psychopathology classification systems. Frontiers in psychology, 6, 1511. https://doi.org/10.3389/fpsyg.2015.01511

Movement Advancement Project (MAP). (2006). Nondiscrimination Laws. Retrieved August 08, 2020, from https://www.lgbtmap.org/equality-maps/non_discrimination_laws

Murphy, M. C., Steele, C. M., & Gross, J. J. (2007). Signaling threat: How situational cues affect women in math, science, and engineering settings. *Psychological Science*, *18*(10), 879–885. http://doi.org/10.1111/j.1467-9280.2007.01995.x

Nash, J. C. (2008). Re-thinking intersectionality. *Feminist Review, 89*(1), 1–15.

Nelson, J. C., Adams, G., & Salter, P. S. (2013). The Marley hypothesis: Denial of racism reflects ignorance of history. *Psychological Science, 24*(2), 213–218. http://doi.org/10.1177/0956797612451466

Newheiser, A.-K., Barreto, M., & Tiemersma, J. (2017). People like me don't belong here: Identity concealment is associated with negative workplace experiences. *Journal of Social Issues, 73*(2), 341–358. http://doi.org/10.1111/josi.12220

Nier, J. A., & Gaertner, S. L. (2012). The challenge of detecting contemporary forms of discrimination. *Journal of Social Issues, 68*(2), 207–220. http://doi.org/10.1111/j.1540-4560.2012.01745.x

Nobles, W. W. (1991). African philosophy: Foundations of Black psychology. In R. L Jones (Ed.), Black psychology (3rd ed.). Berkeley, CA: Cobb & Henry.

Nouvilas-Pallejà, E., Silván-Ferrero, P., Apodaca, M. J. F.-R. D., & Molero, F. (2018). Stigma consciousness and subjective well-being in lesbians and gays. *Journal of Happiness Studies, 19*(4), 1115–1133. http://doi.org/10.1007/s10902-017-9862-1

Novak, N. L., Geronimus, A. T., & Martinez-Cardoso, A. M. (2017). Change in birth outcomes among infants born to Latina mothers after a major immigration raid. *International Journal of Epidemiology, 46*(3), 839–849. http://doi.org/10.1093/ije/dyw346

Obama, M. (2014, January 16). Remarks by the President and First Lady at College Opportunity Summit. Retrieved from https://obamawhitehouse

.archives.gov/realitycheck/the-press-office/2014/01/16/remarks-presi dent-and-first-lady-college-opportunity-summit

Olson, K. R., Durwood, L., Demeules, M., & Mclaughlin, K. A. (2016). Mental health of transgender children who are supported in their identities. *Pediatrics*, *137*(3). http://doi.org/10.1542/peds.2015-3223

Oluo, I. (2019). *So you want to talk about race*. New York, NY Seal Press.

Page-Gould, E., Mendoza-Denton, R., & Tropp, L. R. (2008). With a little help from my cross-group friend: Reducing anxiety in intergroup contexts through cross-group friendship. *Journal of Personality and Social Psychology*, *95*(5), 1080–1094. http://doi.org/10.1037/0022-3514.95.5.1080

Parker, K., Horowitz, J., & Mahl, B. (2016). On Views of Race and Inequality, Blacks and Whites are Worlds Apart: About Four-in-ten Blacks are Doubtful that the US Will Ever Achieve Racial Equality. Pew Research Center.

Paluck, E. L., Shepherd, H., & Aronow, P. M. (2016). Changing climates of conflict: A social network experiment in 56 schools. *Proceedings of the National Academy of Sciences*, *113*(3), 566–571. http://doi.org/10.1073 /pnas.1514483113

Perez-Brumer, A., Day, J. K., Russell, S. T., & Hatzenbuehler, M. L. (2017). Prevalence and correlates of suicidal ideation among transgender youth in California: Findings from a representative, population-based sample of high school students. *Journal of the American Academy of Child & Adolescent Psychiatry*, *56*(9), 739–746. http://doi.org/10.1016/j.jaac.2017.06.010

Phillips, L. T., & Lowery, B. S. (2015). The hard-knock life? Whites claim hardships in response to racial inequity. *Journal of Experimental Social Psychology*, *61*, 12–18.

(2018). Herd invisibility: The psychology of racial privilege. *Current Directions in Psychological Science*, *27*(3), 156–162. http://doi.org/10 .1016/j.jesp.2015.06.008

Phinney, J. S., & Ong, A. D. (2007). Conceptualization and measurement of ethnic identity: Current status and future directions. *Journal of Counseling Psychology*, *54*(3), 271–281. http://doi.org/10.1037/0022-0167.54.3.271

Pincus, F. L. (1996). Discrimination comes in many forms: Individual, institutional, and structural. *American Behavioral Scientist*, *40*(2), 186–194. http://doi.org/10.1177/0002764296040002009

Pinto, R. M., Melendez, R. M., & Spector, A. Y. (2008). Male-to-female transgender individuals building social support and capital from within a gender-focused network. Journal of Gay & Lesbian Social Services: Issues in Practice, Policy & Research, 20(3), 203–220. "https://psycnet.apa.org/doi/10.1080/10538720802235179" https://doi.org/ 10.1080/10538720802235179

Poteat, T., Malik, M., Scheim, A., & Elliott, A. (2017). HIV prevention among transgender populations: knowledge gaps and evidence for action. Current HIV/AIDS Reports, 14(4), 141–152. https://doi.org/10.1007/s11904-017-0360-1

Poteat, T., Wirtz, A., Malik, M., Cooney, E., Cannon, C., Hardy, W. D., ... & Yamanis, T. (2019). A gap between willingness and uptake: findings from mixed methods research on HIV prevention among black and Latina transgender women. *JAIDS Journal of Acquired Immune Deficiency Syndromes, 82(2)*, 131–140. https://doi.org/10.1097/QAI.0000000000002112

Priest, N., Paradies, Y., Trenerry, B., Truong, M., Karlsen, S., & Kelly, Y. (2013). A systematic review of studies examining the relationship between reported racism and health and wellbeing for children and young people. *Social Science & Medicine, 95*, 115–127. http://doi.org/10.1016/j.socscimed.2012.11.031

Purdie-Greenaway, V. (2018, March) *The face of psychology departments worldwide: How diverse are we really?* Paper presented at the Society for Personality and Social Psychology Annual Meeting, Atlanta, Georgia.

Purdie-Vaughns, V., Steele, C. M., Davies, P. G., Ditlmann, R., & Crosby, J. R. (2008). Social identity contingencies: How diversity cues signal threat or safety for African Americans in mainstream institutions. *Journal of Personality and Social Psychology, 94*(4), 615–630. http://doi.org/10.1037/0022-3514.94.4.615

Quintana, S. M. (2007). Racial and ethnic identity: Developmental perspectives and research *Journal of Counseling Psychology, 54*(3), 259–270. http://doi.org/10.1037/0022-0167.54.3.259

Ramsey, G. P. (2003). *Race music: Black cultures from bebop to hip-hop* (Vol. 7). Berkeley, CA University of California Press.

Reimer, N. K., Becker, J. C., Benz, A., Christ, O., Dhont, K., Klocke, U., ... Hewstone, M. (2017). Intergroup contact and social change. *Personality and Social Psychology Bulletin, 43*(1), 121–136. http://doi.org/10.1177/0146167216676478

Rheinschmidt-Same, M., John-Henderson, N. A., & Mendoza-Denton, R. (2017). Ethnically-based theme house residency and expected discrimination predict downstream markers of inflammation among college students. *Social Psychological and Personality Science, 8*(1), 102–111. http://doi.org/10.1177/1948550616662130

Rivas-Drake, D., Seaton, E. K., Markstrom, C., Quintana, S., Syed, M., Lee, R. M., ... & Ethnic and Racial Identity in the 21st Century Study Group. (2014a). Ethnic and racial identity in adolescence: Implications for psychosocial, academic, and health outcomes. *Child Development, 85*(*1*), 40–57. http://doi.org/10.1111/cdev.12200

Rivas-Drake, D., Syed, M., Umaña-Taylor, A., Markstrom, C., French, S., Schwartz, S. J., ... & Ethnic and Racial Identity in the 21st Century Study Group. (2014b). Feeling good, happy, and proud: A meta-analysis of positive ethnic–racial affect and adjustment. *Child Development, 85* (1),77–102. http://doi.org/10.1111/cdev.12175

Rivera, S. (2013). Queens in exile, the forgotten ones. In Street Transvestite Action Revolutionaries: Survival, Revolt, and Queer Antagonist Struggle. Untorelli Press. https://untorellipress.noblogs.org/files/2011/12/STAR.pdf

Rood, B. A., Maroney, M. R., Puckett, J. A., Berman, A. K., Reisner, S. L., & Pantalone, D. W. (2017). Identity concealment in transgender adults: A qualitative assessment of minority stress and gender affirmation. *American Journal of Orthopsychiatry, 87*(6), 704–713. http://doi.org/10 .1037/ort0000303

Russell, S. T., Pollitt, A. M., Li, G., & Grossman, A. H. (2018). Chosen name use is linked to reduced depressive symptoms, suicidal ideation, and suicidal behavior among transgender youth. *Journal of Adolescent Health, 63*(4), 503–505. http://doi.org/10.1016/j .jadohealth.2018.02.003

Salter, P. S., Adams, G., & Perez, M. J. (2018). Racism in the structure of everyday worlds: A cultural-psychological perspective. *Current Directions in Psychological* Science, *27*(3), 150–155. http://doi.org/10 .1177/0963721417724239

Samuels, R., Stanley-Becker, I., & Janes, C. (2019, November 27). Pete Buttigieg says being gay helps him relate to the black struggle. Some reject that notion. The Washington Post. Retrieved from https://www.washington post.com/politics/pete-buttigeg-says-being-gay-helps-him-relate-to-the-black-struggle-some-reject-that-notion/2019/11/27/a29b48ec-113a-11ea-b0fc-62cc38411ebb_story.html

Schmader, T., & Sedikides, C. (2018). State authenticity as fit to environment: The implications of social identity for fit, authenticity, and self-segregation. *Personality and Social Psychology Review, 22*(3), 228–259. http://doi.org/10 .1177/1088868317734080

Schneider, B., & Stoller, N. (1995). Women Resisting AIDS: Feminist Strategies of Empowerment. Temple University Press. Retrieved August 9, 2020, from www.jstor.org/stable/j.ctt14bssgk

Seelman, K. L. (2016). Transgender adults' access to college bathrooms and housing and the relationship to suicidality. *Journal of Homosexuality, 63* (10), 1378–1399. http://doi.org/10.1080/00918369.2016.1157998

Sellers, R. M., Smith, M. A., Shelton, J. N., Rowley, S. A., & Chavous, T. M. (1998). Multidimensional model of racial identity: A reconceptualization of African American racial identity. *Personality and Social Psychology Review*, *2*(1), 18–39. http://doi.org/10.1207/s15327957pspr0201_2

Shapiro, E. (2008). "Trans" cending barriers. *Journal of Gay & Lesbian Social Services*, *16*(3–4), 165–179. http://doi.org/10.1300/j041v16n03_11

Shelton, J. N., Yip, T., Eccles, J. S., Chatman, C. M., Fuligni, A., & Wong,C. (2005). Ethnic identity as a buffer of psychological adjustment tostress. In G. Downey, J. S. Eccles, & C. M. Chatman (Eds.), Navigatingthe future: Social identity, coping, and life tasks (pp. 96–115). NewYork: Russell Sage Foundation

Silva, D. T. D., Bouris, A., Voisin, D., Hotton, A., Brewer, R., & Schneider, J. (2019). Social networks moderate the syndemic effect of psychosocial and structural factors on HIV risk among young Black transgender women and men who have sex with men. *AIDS and Behavior*, *24*(1), 192–205. http://doi.org/10.1007/s10461-019-02575-9

Sotomayor, S. (2013). My beloved world. New York, NY: Alfred Knopf Incorporated.

Smalley, K. B., Warren, J. C., & Barefoot, K. N. (2016). Differences in health risk behaviors across understudied LGBT subgroups. *Health Psychology*, *35*(2), 103–114. http://doi.org/10.1037/hea0000231

Smith, T. B., & Silva, L. (2011). Ethnic identity and personal well-being of people of color: A meta-analysis. Journal of Counseling Psychology, 58(1), 42–60. https://doi.org/10.1037/a0021528

Snapshot: LGBT Equality by State. (n.d.). Retrieved from www.lgbtmap.org /equality-maps

Snibbe, A. C., & Markus, H. R. (2005). You can't always get what you want: Educational attainment, agency, and choice. *Journal of Personality and Social Psychology*, *88*(4), 703–720. http://doi.org/10.1037/0022-3514.88.4.703

Spears Brown, C., & Bigler, R. S. (2005). Children's perceptions of discrimination: A developmental model. *Child Development*, *76*(3), 533–553. http://doi.org/10.1111/j.1467-8624.2005.00862.x

Spencer, S. J., Logel, C., & Davies, P. G. (2016). Stereotype threat. *Annual Review of Psychology*, *67*, 415–437. http://doi.org/10.1146/annurev-psych -073115-103235

Spencer, M. B., Noll, E., Stoltzfus, J., & Harpalani, V. (2001). Identity and school adjustment: Revisiting the "acting White" assumption. Educational Psychologist, 36(1), 21–30. https://doi.org/10.1207/S15326985EP3601_3

Steele, C. M. (2011). *Whistling Vivaldi: How stereotypes affect us and what we can do*. New York: W.W. Norton & Company.

Stephens, N. M., Brannon, T. N., Markus, H. R., & Nelson, J. E. (2015). Feeling at home in college: Fortifying school-relevant selves to reduce social class disparities in higher education. *Social Issues and Policy Review*, 9(1), 1–24. http://doi.org/10.1111/sipr.12008

Stephens, N. M., Dittmann, A. G., & Townsend, S. S. M. (2017). Social class and models of competence: How gateway institutions disadvantage working-class Americans and how to intervene. In C. Dweck, A. Elliot, & D. Yeager (Eds.), Handbook of competence and motivation (2nd ed.): Theory and application. New York, NY: Guilford Press.

Stephens, N. M., Fryberg, S. A., & Markus, H. R. (2011). When choice does not equal freedom: A sociocultural analysis of agency in working-class American contexts. *Social Psychological and Personality Science*, 2(1), 33–41. http://doi.org/10.1177/1948550610378757

Stephens, N. M., Fryberg, S. A., Markus, H. R., Johnson, C. S., & Covarrubias, R. (2012). Unseen disadvantage: How American universities' focus on independence undermines the academic performance of first-generation college students. *Journal of Personality and Social Psychology*, 102(6), 1178–1197. http://doi.org/10.1037/a0027143

Stephens, N. M., Hamedani, M. G., & Destin, M. (2014). Closing the social-class achievement gap: A difference-education intervention improves first-generation students' academic performance and all students' college transition. *Psychological Science*, 25(4), 943–953. http://doi.org/10.1177/0956797613518349

Stephens, N. M., Hamedani, M. G., Markus, H. R., Bergsieker, H. B., & Eloul, L. (2009). Why did they "choose" to stay? Perspectives of Hurricane Katrina observers and survivors. *Psychological Science*, 20(7), 878–886. http://doi.org/10.1111/j.1467-9280.2009.02386.xStephens, N. M., Markus, H. R., & Fryberg, S. A. (2012). Social class disparities in health and education: Reducing inequality by applying a sociocultural self model of behavior. *Psychological Review*, 119(4), 723–744. http://doi.org/10.1037/a0029028

Stephens, N. M., Markus, H. R., & Phillips, L. T. (2014). Social class culture cycles: How three gateway contexts shape selves and fuel inequality. *Annual Review of Psychology*, 65, 611–634. http://doi.org/10.1146/annurev-psych-010213-115143

Stephens, N. M., Markus, H. R., & Townsend, S. S. (2007). Choice as an act of meaning: The case of social class. *Journal of Personality and Social Psychology*, 93(5), 814–830. http://doi.org/10.1037/0022-3514.93.5.814

Stephens, N. M., & Townsend, S. S. (2013). Rank is not enough: Why we need a sociocultural perspective to understand social class. *Psychological Inquiry*, 24(2), 126–130. http://doi.org/10.1080/1047840X.2013.795099

Stewart, T. L., Latu, I. M., Branscombe, N. R., Phillips, N. L., & Denney, H. T. (2012). White privilege awareness and efficacy to reduce racial inequality improve White Americans' attitudes toward African Americans. *Journal of Social Issues, 68*, 11–27. http://doi.org/10.1111/j.1540-4560.2012.01733.x

Strauss, V. (2019, January 24). CDC: Nearly 2 percent of high school students identify as transgender – and more than one-third of them attempt suicide. Retrieved from https://www.washingtonpost.com/education/2019/01/24/ cdc-nearly-percent-high-school-students-identify-transgender-more-than-one-third-them-attempt-suicide/

Sue, D. W. (2010). *Microaggressions in everyday life: Race, gender, and sexual orientation.* Hoboken, NJ John Wiley & Sons.

Sue, D. W., Alsaidi, S., Awad, M. N., Glaeser, E., Calle, C. Z., & Mendez, N. (2019). Disarming racial microaggressions: Microintervention strategies for targets, White allies, and bystanders. *American Psychologist, 74*(1), 128–142. http://doi.org/10.1037/amp0000296

Sue, D. W., Capodilupo, C. M., Torino, G. C., Bucceri, J. M., Holder, A., Nadal, K. L., & Esquilin, M. (2007). Racial microaggressions in everyday life: Implications for clinical practice. *American Psychologist, 62*(4), 271–286. http://doi.org/10.1037/0003-066X.62.4.271

Sullivan, A. (2020, March 20). How to survive a plague. New York Magazine. Retrieved from https://nymag.com/intelligencer/2020/03/andrew-sulli van-how-to-survive-the-coronavirus-pandemic.html

Swank, E., Woodford, M. R., & Lim, C. (2013). Antecedents of pro-LGBT advocacy among sexual minority and heterosexual college students. *Sexuality Research and Social Policy, 10*(4), 317–332. http://doi.org/10 .1007/s13178-013-0136-3

Swim, J. K., Hyers, L. L., Cohen, L. L., & Ferguson, M. J. (2001). Everyday sexism: Evidence for its incidence, nature, and psychological impact from three daily diary studies. *Journal of Social Issues, 57*(1), 31–53. http://doi .org/10.1111/0022-4537.00200

Tajfel, H., Turner, J. C. (1986). An integrative theory of group conflict. In Austin, W. G., Worchel, S. (Eds.), The social psychology of intergroup relations (pp. 7–24). Chicago, IL: Nelson-Hall.

Tatum, B. D. (2017). *Why are all the Black kids sitting together in the cafe-teria?: And other conversations about race.* New York: Basic Books.

Taylor, V. J., Brannon, T. N., & Valladares, J. V. (2019). Intergroup conflict through a sociocultural lens: How collective histories and memories impact present-day intergroup understandings and misunderstandings. In S. Mukherjee and P. S. Salter (Eds.), History and collective memory from the margins: A global perspective. (pp. 3–30). Hauppauge, NY: Nova Publishers.

Tozer, E. E., & Hayes, J. A. (2004). Why do individuals seek conversion therapy? *The Counseling Psychologist, 32*(5), 716–740. http://doi.org/10.1177/0011000004267563

Turban, J. L., Beckwith, N., Reisner, S. L., & Keuroghlian, A. S. (2019). Association between recalled exposure to gender identity conversion efforts and psychological distress and suicide attempts among transgender adults. *JAMA Psychiatry, 77*(1), 1–9. http://doi.org/10.1001/jamapsychiatry.2019.2285

Unzueta, M. M., & Binning, K. R. (2012). Diversity is in the eye of the beholder: How concern for the in-group affects perceptions of racial diversity. *Personality and Social Psychology Bulletin, 38*(1), 26–38. http://doi.org/10.1177/0146167211418528

Valdiserri, R. O., Holtgrave, D. R., Poteat, T. C., & Beyrer, C. (2019). Unraveling Health Disparities Among Sexual and Gender Minorities: A Commentary on the Persistent Impact of Stigma. Journal of Homosexuality, 66(5), 571–589. https://doi.org/10.1080/00918369.2017.1422944

Vaid, U. (1995). Virtual equality: The mainstreaming of gay and lesbian liberation. New York, NY: Anchor Books.

Venn-Brown, A. (2007). *A life of unlearning: A journey to find the truth.* Australia New Holland Publishers.

Walton, G. M. (2014). The new science of wise psychological interventions. *Current Directions in Psychological Science, 23*(1), 73–82. http://doi.org/10.1177/0963721413512856

Walton, G., & Cohen, G. (2007). A question of belonging: Rrace, social fit, and achievement. *Journal of Personality and Social Psychology*, 92(1), 82–96. http://doi.org/10.1037/0022-3514.92.1.82

(2011). A brief social-belonging intervention improves academic and health outcomes of minority students. *Science, 331*(6023), 1447–1451. http://doi.org/10.1126/science.1198364

Walton, G. M., & Wilson, T. D. (2018). Wise interventions: Psychological remedies for social and personal problems. *Psychological Review, 125*(5), 617–655. http://doi.org/10.1037/rev0000115

Webster, L. (2019). "I am I": Self-constructed transgender identities in internet-mediated forum communication. *International Journal of the Sociology of Language*, 256, 129–146. http://doi.org/10.1515/ijsl-2018-2015

Wernick, L. J. (2012). Privilege: Organizing young people with wealth to support social justice. *Social Service Review, 86*(2), 323–345. http://doi.org/10.1086/666874

Wernick, L. J., Kulick, A., & Chin, M. (2017). Gender identity disparities in bathroom safety and wellbeing among high school students. Journal of youth and adolescence, 46(5), 917–930. doi: 10.1007/s10964-017-0652-1

Wessel, J. (2017). The Importance of Allies and Allied Organizations: Sexual Orientation Disclosure and Concealment at Work. *Journal of Social Issues. 73.* 240–254. 10.1111/josi.12214.

Williams, D. P., Joseph, N., Hill, L. K., Sollers III, J. J., Vasey, M. W., Way, B. M., ... & Thayer, J. F. (2019). Stereotype threat, trait perseveration, and vagal activity: Evidence for mechanisms underpinning health disparities in Black Americans. *Ethnicity & Health, 24*(8), 909–926. http://doi.org/10.1080/13557858.2017.1378803

Woodford, M. R., Kulick, A., Garvey, J. C., Sinco, B. R., & Hong, J. S. (2018). LGBTQ policies and resources on campus and the experiences and psychological well-being of sexual minority college students: Advancing research on structural inclusion. *Psychology of Sexual Orientation and Gender Diversity, 5*(4), 445–456. http://doi.org/10.1037/sgd0000289

Wong, C. F., Schrager, S. M., Holloway, I. W., Meyer, I. H., & Kipke, M. D. (2014). Minority stress experiences and psychological well-being: The impact of support from and connection to social networks within the Los Angeles house and ball communities. Prevention Science, 15(1), 44–55. doi: 10.1007/s11121-012-0348-4.

Worthen, M. G. F. (2017). "Gay equals White"? Racial, ethnic, and sexual identities and attitudes toward LGBT individuals among college students at a Bible Belt university. *The Journal of Sex Research, 55*(8), 995–1011. http://doi.org/10.1080/00224499.2017.1378309

Yeager, D. S., & Walton, G. M. (2011). Social-psychological interventions in education: They're not magic. *Review of Educational Research, 81*(2), 267–301. http://doi.org/10.3102/0034654311405999

Young, A., & Jay, K. (1992). *Out of the closets: Voices of gay liberation.* New York: New York University Press.

Acknowledgments

We would like to acknowledge the research assistance and support of the members of the Culture and Contact Lab at the University of California, Los Angeles.

Cambridge Elements ≡

Applied Social Psychology

Susan Clayton
College of Wooster, Ohio

Susan Clayton is a social psychologist at the College of Wooster in Wooster, Ohio. Her research focuses on the human relationship with nature, how it is socially constructed, and how it can be utilized to promote environmental concern.

About the Series
Many social psychologists have used their research to understand and address pressing social issues, from poverty and prejudice to work and health. Each Element in this series reviews a particular area of applied social psychology. Elements will also discuss applications of the research findings and describe directions for future study.

Cambridge Elements ☰

Applied Social Psychology

Elements in the Series

Printed in the United States
By Bookmasters